# A TUDOR CHRISTMAS

To our families, who have always
made Christmas so magical

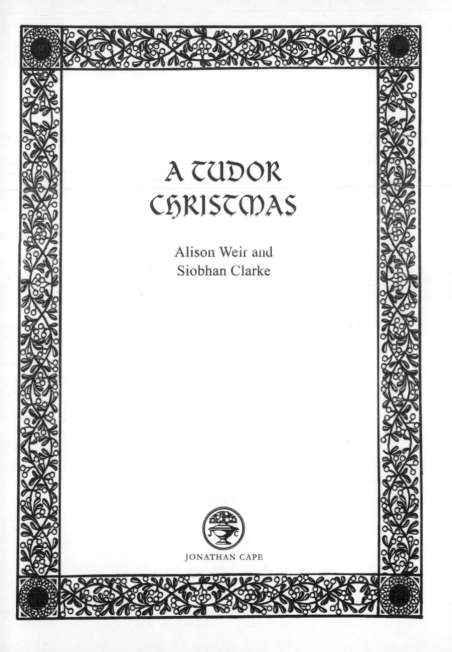

# A TUDOR CHRISTMAS

Alison Weir and
Siobhan Clarke

JONATHAN CAPE

1 3 5 7 9 10 8 6 4 2

Jonathan Cape, an imprint of Vintage,
20 Vauxhall Bridge Road,
London SW1V 2SA

Jonathan Cape is part of the Penguin Random House group of companies
whose addresses can be found at global.penguinrandomhouse.com.

Penguin
Random House
UK

Inside illustrations ©  Bill Sanderson

First published by Jonathan Cape in 2018

penguin.co.uk/vintage

A CIP catalogue record for this book is available from the British Library

ISBN 9781787330641

Printed and bound in Great Britain by Clays Ltd, Elcograf S.p.A.

Penguin Random House is committed to a sustainable future for
our business, our readers and our planet. This book is made from
Forest Stewardship Council® certified paper.

MIX
Paper from
responsible sources
FSC® C018179

... but here a jolly
Verse crown'd with ivy and with holly;
That tells of winter's tales and mirth
That milk-maids make about the hearth;
Of Christmas sports, the wassail-bowl,
That toss'd up, after Fox-i'-th'-hole;
Of Blind-man-buff, and of the care
That young men have to Shoe the Mare;
Of Twelfth-tide cakes, of peas and beans,
Wherewith ye make those merry scenes,
Whenas ye choose your king and queen,
And cry out, 'Hey for our town green!'
Of ash-heaps, in the which ye use
Husbands and wives by streaks to choose;
Of crackling laurel, which fore-sounds
A plenteous harvest to your grounds;
Of these, and such like things, for shift,
We send instead of New-year's gift.
Read then, and when your faces shine
With buxom meat and cap'ring wine,
Remember us in cups full crown'd,
And let our city-health go round,
Quite through the young maids and the men,
To the ninth number, if not ten;
Until the fired chestnuts leap
For joy to see the fruits ye reap,
From the plump chalice and the cup
That tempts till it be tossed up.

Then as ye sit about your embers,
Call not to mind those fled Decembers;
But think on these, that are t' appear,
As daughters to the instant year;
Sit crown'd with rose-buds, and carouse,
Till LIBER PATER twirls the house
About your ears, and lay upon
The year, your cares, that's fled and gone:
And let the russet swains the plough
And harrow hang up resting now;
And to the bag-pipe all address,
Till sleep takes place of weariness.
And thus throughout, with Christmas plays,
Frolic the full twelve holy-days.

Robert Herrick, 'A New Year's Gift to Sir Simeon Steward', 1628

# CONTENTS

'When Christmastide
comes in like a bride'

# INTRODUCTION

All hail to the days that merit more praise
Than all the rest of the year,
And welcome the nights that double delights,
As well for the poor as the peer!
Good fortune attend each merry man's friend,
That doth but the best that he may;
Forgetting old wrongs, with carols and songs,
To drive the cold winter away.

This time of the year is spent in good cheer,
And neighbours together do meet,

To sit by the fire, with friendly desire,
Each other in love do greet;
Old grudges forgot, are put in the pot,
All sorrows aside they lay,
The old and the young doth carol his song,
To drive the cold winter away.

To mask and to mum kind neighbours will come
With wassails of nut-brown ale,
To drink and carouse to all in the house,
As merry as bucks in the dale;
Where cake, bread and cheese is brought for your fees,
To make you the longer stay;
At the fire to warm will do you no harm,
To drive the cold winter away.

When Christmastide comes in like a bride,
With holly and ivy clad,
Twelve days in the year, much mirth and good cheer,
In every household is had;
The country guise is then to devise
Some gambols of Christmas play,
Whereat the young men do best that they can,
To drive the cold winter away.

When white-bearded frost hath threatened his worst,
And fallen from branch and brier,
Then time away calls, from husbandry halls

And from the good countryman's fire,
Together to go to plough and to sow,
To get us both food and array;
And thus with content the time we have spent
To drive the cold winter away.

For at least five thousand years, the depth of winter has been a time for merrymaking and conviviality, 'to drive the cold winter away', as one popular Jacobean song had it. Many of the major world religions have festivals of light to counteract the darkest season of the year, and Christmas is one of the greatest, most splendid and most loved of them all.

For many people, it is a season of special celebration and festivity, a spiritual journey of peace and hope, a magical time of tradition and mystery. It can involve weeks of preparation, decoration, cooking and entertaining. In Tudor England, things were much the same. We might think that our modern Christmas derives largely from the Victorians, who popularised Christmas trees, Christmas cards and Father Christmas, but in fact many of our traditions – such as eating mince pies, singing carols and kissing under the mistletoe – date back to Tudor times and beyond. In these pages, you can discover more about these, as well as encountering other customs that have fallen into disuse, from the Lords of Misrule to the Queen of the Pea.

In Tudor times, as today people enjoyed a good dinner and special festive fare. They went to church on Christmas morning,

3

opened up their houses to family and friends, ate and drank as much as they could afford, gathered around the fire roasting chestnuts, played games, danced, told ghost stories and exchanged gifts. Christmas, as described in 1623 by Lancelot Andrews, Bishop of Winchester, was a time for 'gathering together, neighbourly meetings and invitations, good housekeeping and hospitality'. For this short, enchanting season, everyday cares were set aside and the emphasis was on everyone enjoying themselves.

The history of Christmas does not begin with Christ, as our Christmas rituals evolved from pagan rites. Pagan peoples celebrated the winter solstice – the shortest day of the year. The winter solstice was immensely important at a time when communities could not be certain of living through the winter. When the hours of darkness were at their longest, the solstice was a turning point, bringing with it the promise that soon the days would grow longer and the sun would return, warming the earth and bringing new life and hope. The fourth-century Christian Church adopted 21 December, the day of the winter solstice, as the feast day of St Thomas the Apostle.

Northern Europeans called the solstice 'Jul' – a term remembered in the English word Yule, which now means Christmas. Yule marked the death of one year and the birth of the next. It is also associated with the ancient legendary fertility figure of the Green Man, or 'Ing', who represents rebirth. The symbol of Ing is the boar, and in ancient times, a boar's head was traditionally served on a bed of greenery on Midwinter Day.

Long before the Middle Ages, old pagan traditions were absorbed into Christian festivals. The actual date of Christ's birth is unknown, but the fact that Christmas falls around the same time as the winter solstice and the ancient Roman festival of Saturnalia is no coincidence. Saturnalia was celebrated from 17 to 23 December; Saturn being the Roman god of fertility, it was the occasion for riotous feasting, drunkenness, mischief-making, games and orgies, a time when formal roles were reversed, with masters waiting upon slaves, and a 'king' was chosen to keep rule over the festivities. Many of those elements remained part of the Christmas tradition.

The birth of the popular Roman god Mithras was celebrated on 25 December, and in AD 354, the Emperor Aurelian decreed that this day be named Natalis Solis Invicti, to celebrate the birth of the pagan sun god Sol. Some scholars have suggested that this festival was also adopted by the Christian Church, to commemorate the Nativity, but in the oldest-surviving Christian chronology, written in AD 221, the historian Julius Africanus postulated that Jesus was conceived on 25 March, which later became known as Lady Day, after the Virgin Mary's miraculous conception. Since 25 December fell nine months later, it is no surprise that that date was adopted as Christmas Day well before the end of the third century, and recognised by the Roman Church in the fourth century.

The prominence of Christmas increased gradually after Charlemagne was crowned Roman Emperor on Christmas Day 800. The Saxon King Edmund the Martyr was anointed on Christmas Day 855 and William the Conqueror was crowned king of England on Christmas Day 1066. As the infant Jesus entered the world to create His holy kingdom at this time, so it was deemed an auspicious time for earthly kings to begin a reign.

The traditional English Christmas has its origins in the ninth century, when King Alfred the Great enshrined in law the importance of keeping the Church's feasts, and commanded that there should be a holiday on Christmas Day and the twelve days that followed, for it was believed that the Magi had journeyed for twelve days to see the infant Jesus. During that period, no free man could be compelled to work. From that time, the common man has enjoyed this right to the best of his ability, while kings and nobles have indulged themselves in abundance on a lordly scale.

In 1038, we find the first use of the word Christmas, when it was called 'Christ's Mass' in an Anglo-Saxon text.

By the high Middle Ages, Christmas had become so prominent that chroniclers routinely noted where various magnates kept, or celebrated, it. It was traditional for medieval kings and queens to wear their crowns at the solemn feast of Christmas, and the Tudor monarchs carried on this custom at New Year. Their court was at its most splendid on the feast days that marked this major religious celebration: Christmas Day, New Year, Twelfth Night and the feast of the Epiphany.

By Tudor times, preparations for the Yuletide season often began weeks in advance. The forty days before Christmas were called the 'forty days of St Martin', or Advent, which was the season of expectation and atonement. Martinmas – the feast of St Martin of Tours – on 11 November marked the traditional beginning of winter, and was seen by many as the commencement of the Christmas season, while others began preparing for Christmas on 1 November, All Saints' Day.

Thomas Kirchmaier (1511–63), a Lutheran pastor in

Straubingen, Bavaria, wrote plays and poems that were performed and published in England. In them, he described the excitement of the run-up to Christmas:

> Three weeks before the day whereon was born the Lord of grace,
> And on the Thursday, boys and girls do run in every place,
> And bounce and beat at every door, with blows and lusty snaps,
> And cry the advent of the Lord, not born as yet, perhaps:
> And wishing to the neighbours all, that in the houses dwell,
> A happy year, and everything to spring and prosper well:
> Here have they pears, and plums, and pence; each man gives willingly

The devout were supposed to fast in Advent, the period of preparation and atonement that ended on Christmas Eve. The twelve days of Christmas, known as Christmastide, were celebrated from Christmas Day, 25 December, until Twelfth Night, 5 January. Each day represented one of the twelve months of the passing year. For agricultural workers, Christmas extended to Plough Monday, the first Monday after Epiphany on 6 January, when they went back to work. The twelve days were all celebrated, but not equally: the chief ones were Christmas Day, New Year's Day, Twelfth Night, and the feast of Epiphany, when the celebrations reached their climax.

For many, Christmas offered a welcome respite from the daily toil and grinding poverty of the rest of the year. In 1577, William Harrison, an Essex clergyman, published his *Description of England*, in which he described the poor as farm workers, servants and vagrants, who have 'neither voice nor authority'. England was overwhelmingly a farming society of small communities, where people worked extremely hard, six days a week, just to survive. Only a very small proportion of people lived in towns, probably not more than one in twenty.

Life could be hard. Mortality rates were high; the average life expectancy was around forty years, as medical knowledge was limited, and many children died young. For some, the grinding poverty of a daily existence that meant starvation might be a real prospect. Winters were more severe than they are today; the sixteenth century witnessed a mini ice age that would last for two hundred years. Yet a quarter of all the households in the country had servants, which meant that even humble people employed them, as well as the titled and wealthy.

Boys and men were kept busy with ploughing, hedging, carting and the heavy work of the harvest. The women kept house, prepared meals, made butter, cheese, bread, beer, candles and medicines, and looked after livestock. Small children might earn a penny bird-scaring or minding sheep.

The government controlled rates of pay and even the hours of work. The Elizabethan Statute of Labourers, passed in 1562, laid down that 'all artificers and labourers' had to work from 5 a.m. to 7 or 8 p.m., except between September and March, when they laboured through the hours of daylight. So a labourer could expect to work from sunrise to sunset in the winter, and from sunrise to early evening in the summer. Sundays and major saints' days were holidays, and much cherished, as were the twelve days of Christmas, when all work except the tending of animals was forbidden, and spinning wheels were threaded with flowers and greenery so that women could not use them.

Christmas was one of the four annual 'Quarter Days', which may, or may not, have been a reason for cheer. They fell on Lady Day (25 March), Midsummer Day (24 June), Michaelmas (29 September) and Christmas (25 December). On Quarter Days, servants' contracts began and ended, and rent was due from tenants.

Considering the daily toil of everyday life, it is unsurprising that the Christmas season was so important, and indeed magical, to ordinary people, affording them free time for leisure, games and entertainments, and better food for those whose usual diet was coarse bread, soups and the staple food of pottage (which was made by boiling vegetables, grains and, if available, meat or fish). Meat was a luxury, although cheap salt beef was eaten in virtually every Tudor household, and pork was also eaten, since many people owned, or had shares in, a pig. Expensive spices and sugar were generally out of reach to the common man, although honey might be used for sweetening dishes, and there would be fresh berries and fruit in season. The possibility of eating some richer, more appetising foods at Christmas, in contrast to the usual plain diet, would have been eagerly anticipated by the less well-off.

By contrast, seasonal spending at court was lavish. Henry VIII's expenses for the first Christmas of his reign in 1509 show that the nineteen-year-old King outlaid the equivalent of a staggering £13.5m. His total revenue for the year was £16.5m. The money went on food, entertainment and gifts. Beneficiaries included choirboys, musicians, actors and servants. The King paid his blind court poet, Master Bernard André, £5 – the equivalent of £2,400 in today's money – and another £1, now £483, to a woman who brought a pomander (perfumed ball) to the palace to keep the air fresh.

The ballad referred to at the beginning of this chapter, called 'All Hail to the Days', first appeared in a broadside of *c*.1625, where it is described as 'A Pleasant Country New Ditty: Merrily shewing how to drive the cold winter away'. It may post-date the Tudor era, but little had changed between 1603 and 1625, and it certainly captures the essence of a Tudor Christmas.

In this book, we will be exploring all the fascinating aspects of a Tudor Christmas: how it was kept by ordinary people, and how the court celebrated, for what happened at court had a strong influence on what happened elsewhere. The Tudor period was an age of momentous and divisive religious change, with the Reformation of the 1530s severing ties with the Pope and the Church of Rome, and the establishment in 1559, under Elizabeth I, of the Protestant Anglican Church; and it is interesting to explore how this impacted on the way people celebrated Christmas.

We have also broadened the scope of the book to embrace the pagan and medieval origins of the various customs, and to look at what transpired in the seventeenth century – when England became a Puritan republic – to interrupt the centuries-old traditional celebration of Christmas, and how those observances were preserved.

Our book is loosely structured around the twelve days of Christmas, and in each day/chapter we explore a different popular feature of the Tudor Christmas in more depth. We have based our chapter titles on the imagined children of Father Christmas, in *Christmas, His Masque*, by the playwright Ben Jonson, because their names reflect the various aspects of Yuletide: Misrule, Carol, Mince-Pie, Gambol, Post and Pair (after a card game), New Year's Gift, Mumming, Wassail, Offering and Baby-Cake. (The meaning of some of these names will become clear in the text.) Because there are only ten 'children', we have taken quotes from the masque for the other chapter headings.

Throughout the text, you will find poems and carols that evoke the spirit of the festive season in Tudor England, and describe in their own unique ways the various customs and celebrations. We have also included recipes in their original form, although anyone attempting to follow them should be aware that tastes may not appeal to a modern palate, some ingredients are not easy to come by, and quantities may be gargantuan! Today, we do not have the large halls and kitchens of our wealthier forebears that facilitated such grand-scale celebrating, but you might be surprised at how many of their traditions still survive in one form or another.

Then, as now, it was the spirit of the season that made it so magical, as the chorister, farmer and poet Thomas Tusser evokes in his verses:

Of Christ cometh Christmas, the name with the feast,
A time full of joy to the greatest and least:
At Christmas was Christ (our Saviour) born;
The world through sin altogether forlorn.

At Christmas we banquet, the rich with the poor,
Who then (but the miser) but openeth his door?
At Christmas, of Christ many carols we sing,
And give many gifts in the joy of that King.

24 December
Christmas Eve

FASTING

Bringing home the Yule Log

Come, bring with a noise,
My merry, merry boys,
The Christmas Log to the firing;
While my good Dame, she
Bids ye all be free;
And drink to your heart's desiring.

With the last year's brand
Light the new block, and
For good success in his spending,
On your psaltries play,
That sweet luck may
Come while the log is a-tinding.

Drink now the strong beer,
Cut the white loaf here,
The while the meat is a-shredding;
For the rare mince-pie
And the plums stand by
To fill the paste that's a-kneading.

Robert Herrick, 'Ceremonies for Christmas', *Hesperides*, 1648

ust before Christmas 1536, the Thames froze in London. On 22 December, Henry VIII and his third wife, Jane Seymour, warmly wrapped in furs, rode on horseback from Westminster to the City, which was gaily decorated in their honour with tapestries and cloth of gold; priests in copes with crosiers stood at every street corner waiting to bless the royal party, and despite the bitter cold, large crowds turned out to watch the procession, cheering loudly. After a service in St Paul's to mark the beginning of the Christmas celebrations, Henry and Jane spurred their horses across the frozen river and galloped to the Surrey shore. Then they rode to Greenwich Palace, where they would keep a lavish Christmas court.

# The Advent fast

*'Food for virtue'*

What is more effective than fasting, by which we approach God, and, resisting the devil, we overcome indulgent vices? For fasting has always been food for virtue: chaste thoughts, reasonable desires, and more sound deliberations profit from fasting. And through these voluntary afflictions, our flesh dies to concupiscence and our spirit is renewed for moral excellence.

Pope Leo the Great

If you had woken up on Christmas Eve in Tudor England, before the Reformation of the 1530s, you would have faced a day of fasting, for this was the last day of Advent, a season of penitence in which good Christians prepared themselves spiritually for the coming of Christ. Advent began four weeks before Christmas, and on the Ember Days – the Mondays, Wednesdays and Fridays after the feast of St Lucy on 13 December – the devout were supposed to do penance and fast, avoiding meat, cheese and eggs. Christmas Eve was also a day of fasting and abstinence, but that ended after a final meal of fish had been served, though not before noon. The feasting that would begin on Christmas Day, for which great preparations had been ongoing throughout the fast, would be doubly appreciated after the restricted fare of Advent – though

18

as is clear from a poem by Robert Herrick (1591–1674), some were not prepared to wait that long:

Come, guard this night the Christmas pie,
That the thief, though ne'er so sly,
With his flesh-hooks don't come nigh
    To catch it.
From him who all alone sits there,
Having his eyes still in his ear,
And a deal of nightly fear,
    To watch it.

# Decorations

*'Crown'd with ivy and with holly'*

Because of Advent, tradition demanded that houses were not decorated for the festive season until Christmas Eve. On that day, cloaked and gloved against the cold, adults and children went merrily out in the countryside and into woodlands to gather evergreens such as holly and ivy, which they used to festoon their homes and their local churches. Some was woven around wooden frames and stuck with candles. The Elizabethan annalist John Stow recorded that 'every man's house' was bedecked with holly and ivy. In London, every building, as well as 'the conduits and standards [flagpoles] in the street were likewise garnished', while Queen Elizabeth I herself paid for the churches adjacent to her palaces to be adorned with holly and ivy.

Evergreens had long been deemed miraculous for staying alive while other trees and plants died: they were invested with mystical properties and seen to symbolise eternal life. Carrying evergreens into the house was held to bring good fortune, but doing so before Christmas Eve would invoke bad luck. That superstition dated back to the ancient Druids, who believed that tree spirits dwelt in greenery, and if they had to stay indoors for too long during the dark days of midwinter, they would make mischief for the household.

Holly, ivy and mistletoe had been used since pre-Christian times to celebrate the winter solstice. The ancient Romans observed that the Druids of the British Isles used mistletoe in winter solstice ceremonies and for healing. The philosopher Pliny described a religious rite in which white-clad Druids climbed a sacred oak, cut down the mistletoe growing on it, then sacrificed two white bulls.

Mistletoe was appropriately hung high as a decoration, for it is a parasite and grows in the branches of trees. The custom of hanging a ball of mistletoe from the ceiling and exchanging kisses under it as a sign of friendship and goodwill is an ancient one. According to legend, when enemies met under mistletoe they had to lay down their arms and observe a truce until the next day; this is one explanation of how the custom originated. Another connects it with the Norse goddess Frigg, whose son Baldur was stabbed to death by a sprig of mistletoe. Her tears were turned into the white pearlescent berries of the plant, and she commanded that all who passed under the mistletoe must do no harm, but kiss each other in the spirit of peace and friendship.

Although there was a medieval tradition that Christ's cross had been formed from the wood of the mythical mistletoe tree, churches and abbeys banned mistletoe because of its pagan connections – with one exception: at York Minster, a bunch of mistletoe was laid on the altar every Christmas.

Holly was also considered a sacred plant by the Druids, its evergreen leaves and bright red berries symbolising fertility and eternal life, and its white flowers the purity of the virgin birth and the milk of the Holy Mother. As Christmas gradually replaced Yule, holly became a symbol of Christ's crown of thorns, and it was even claimed that His cross had been made of holly wood. Holly was therefore believed to offer protection against witches and goblins. Prickly holly was seen as a male plant and smooth holly as female; whichever type was brought into the house first dictated who would hold sway in the following year: the master or the mistress. Possibly a certain amount of jostling went on …

William Shakespeare wrote a seasonal song, popularly called 'Shakespeare's Carol', in *As You Like It*, which was first performed in 1603 and mentions the festive holly:

Blow, blow, thou winter wind,
Thou art not so unkind
    As man's ingratitude;
    Thy tooth is not so keen,
Because thou art not seen,
    Although thy breath be rude.

21

Heigh-ho! sing, heigh-ho! unto the green holly:
Most friendship is feigning, most loving mere folly:
Then, heigh-ho, the holly!
    This life is most jolly.

While 'boughs of holly' often decorated the hall, ivy was used mainly to adorn churches, porches and the outsides of houses, possibly because of its association with graveyards, but more likely because it was thought to protect against evil spirits and disaster. It was another ancient evergreen symbol of life, thought of as female, with holly as its male counterpart.

Holly and ivy have been the mainstay of English Christmas decorations in churches since at least the fifteenth century. The purchase of these evergreens is mentioned regularly in urban churchwardens' accounts, while in the countryside, of course, they would have been freely available. The country clergyman and poet Robert Herrick tells us that bays and rosemary also were often 'stuck about the houses and church as Christmas decorations'. 'When other fruits and flowers decay, the bay yet grows full green', ran a rhyme published in 1557 in *Tottel's Miscellany*. Both bay and rosemary were protective plants. Their association with Christmas, as much as that of holly and ivy, was still apparent in the late seventeenth century, but is lost to us today.

The Church was well aware of the pagan connection with evergreens, and in some countries such decorations were banned, but not in England, where the greenery of the season, along with dried fruit, berries and candles, constituted the bulk of Tudor

Christmas decorations. The royal palaces were adorned with 'holly, ivy and bays, and whatsoever the season afforded to be green', and were infused with the scents of Christmas spices – cinnamon, ginger, cloves and nutmeg, which had been popular since they were brought back from the Orient by medieval crusaders. Spices were costly, which was why, for many, they were a treat at Christmas, and why, even today, a lot of Christmas food contains spices. Oranges were used for decoration too – they were being imported in tens of thousands into England by Tudor times. They are at their best in winter, and their shape is symbolic of Christ's dominion over the Earth, which is why they have traditionally been given as gifts.

Although the fir tree had long been a Christian symbol, with its evergreen branches representing eternal life, there were no Christmas trees as we know them in Tudor England. The first, isolated record of a decorated tree in England dates from the fifteenth century, when a fir tree lit with candles was set up in a London street. If there were others, they are not recorded.

Legend has it that the German reformer Martin Luther invented the Christmas tree in the early sixteenth century. One winter's night in 1536, so the story goes, Luther was walking through a pine forest near his home in Wittenberg when he suddenly looked up and saw thousands of stars glinting jewel-like among the branches of the trees. This wondrous sight inspired him to set up a candlelit fir tree in his house that Christmas to remind his children of the starry heavens whence their Saviour came.

But while the custom of decorating a Christmas tree was to flourish in Germany, it did not become popular in England until the nineteenth century. Prior to that, the chief decoration in people's houses was the kissing bough, a ball of greenery made of evergreens such as holly and bay, and sometimes stuck with apples – and always with a sprig of mistletoe; it was constructed on a wooden frame and suspended from the ceiling.

# The Yule log
*'The Christmas brand'*

The poet Robert Herrick had a warm appreciation of the traditions and superstitions of his time, doubtless instilled in his Elizabethan childhood, and this is evident in the evocative poems he wrote about Christmas, which conjure up better than any other the true spirit of the season. A particularly evocative one, 'The Yule Log', dates from *c*.1630 (see page 25).

The pagan tradition of the Yule log – thought to derive from early Viking invaders – was widely observed. The men would go out on Christmas Eve and fell a tree in the woods, then drag the trunk home to the hearth, where the waiting household decorated it with ribbons and greenery, and perhaps kindled it with bindings of ivy and hazel twigs and a good splash of alcohol. At court, this ritual took place in the great hall or presence chamber of the palace. The Yule log was always lit with a piece of wood saved from the one used the previous year, and kept burning throughout the twelve days of Christmas. People believed that if it went out, bad luck would ensue in the following year.

The custom of the Yule log was, however, on the wane. In medieval times, the main room in the house was the hall, where domestic life was lived more or less communally. In the Tudor period, kings – and eventually their subjects – began to value the privacy and warmth of smaller chambers, so that great halls became redundant and houses ceased to be built with them. Gradually, as hearths were reduced in size, Yule logs became smaller and were kept burning for only twelve hours; and thus the custom began to die out.

## Christmas cribs
*'The Babe of Bethlehem'*

For centuries, Christmas cribs had been set up in churches and blessed. These model Nativity scenes had been part of Christmas since at least AD 432, when Pope Sixtus III built what would become one of the most famous Nativities, at the Basilica of Santa Maria Maggiore in Rome, in the underground Chapel of Christmas, which still contains a reliquary said to hold the remains of Jesus's manger. The celebration of a special Mass at midnight on Christmas Eve originated here, for ancient doctrine laid down that Christ had been born at midnight. This Mass became the first of the three celebrated on Christmas Day and was originally known as the Angels' Mass. The highlight of the Midnight Mass for Catholics is the symbolic arrival of the Christ Child, who is represented by the baby placed in the manger.

Cribs became popular with lay folk after 1223, when St Francis created a life-sized manger scene, with people in costume, real animals – an ox and an ass – and a baby of wax, on the hill above the village of Greccio, and himself preached the Gospel story. The custom spread across Europe, and cribs became a much-loved element of Christmas.

# The spirits of the season
*'So hallow'd and so gracious is the time'*

Deep within all the festivity, bustle and good cheer, there lay the quiet heart and purpose of the celebrations. As Christmas Day approached, there was devout expectancy, but also a fearful sense of the supernatural. In Tudor England, spirits were thought to roam free in the darkness during the Christmas season. In 1553, Thomas Kirchmaier wrote of the fear this could engender:

> For these three nights are always thought unfortunate to be,
> Wherein they are afraid of sprites and cankered witches' spite,
> And dreadful devils, black and grim, that then have chiefest might.

Already, in Elizabethan times, there was an established tradition of telling ghost stories by the fireside at Christmas, particularly on Christmas Eve, a thrilling way to while away the hours on dark winter evenings. For centuries, the belief had lingered that the veil between this world and the next was at its thinnest at the time of the winter solstice, the longest night of the year, and that spirits could walk the earth. In 1589, the dramatist Christopher Marlowe, in *The Jew of Malta*, had a character recalling:

Now I remember those old women's words,
Who in my wealth would tell me winter's tales,
And speak of spirits and ghosts that glide by night

And in Shakespeare's *A Winter's Tale*, written in 1611, Prince Mamillius decides to relate one such tale to the court of Sicily:

A sad tale's best for winter: I have one
Of sprites and goblins ...

Yet it was also believed that between Christmas Eve and Twelfth Night, the power of the newborn Christ would outrank that of the spirits and ensure that they brought good luck instead of bad. In Shakespeare's *Hamlet*, Marcellus, having seen the ghost of Hamlet's father, says to Horatio and Bernardo:

Some say that ever 'gainst that season comes
Wherein our Saviour's birth is celebrated,
This bird of dawning singeth all night long;

And then, they say, no spirit dare stir abroad,

The nights are wholesome, then no planets strike,

No fairy takes, nor witch hath power to charm,

So hallow'd and so gracious is the time.

Many believed that, at midnight on Christmas Eve, cattle and oxen would kneel in the dark, worshipping the newly born Christ Child, and bees would come buzzing out of their hives to welcome Him.

Above everything else, the Tudor Christmas was a religious festival, a time when people attended services and made their offerings on the various feast days. It began with the vigil of Christmas Day, when the church bells rang out to invite the people to Midnight Mass. They found the sanctuary lit up with tapers, and the altar with many candles. The clergy's voices would soar as they sang 'Adeste Fideles', and Christmas came in with all its mystery and wonder.

At midnight, after the final meal of Advent, came the first Mass of Christmas Day, when the celebrations could begin, as Kirchmaier describes:

> … at midnight up they rise, and every man to Mass.
>
> This time so holy counted is, that divers earnestly
>
> Do think the waters all to wine are changed suddenly
>
> In that same hour that Christ Himself was born and came to light,
>
> And unto water straight again transformed and altered quite.
>
> This done, a wooden child in clouts is on the altar set,
>
> About the which both boys and girls do dance and trimly get,

And carols sing in praise of Christ, and for to help them here,
The organs answer every verse with sweet and solemn cheer.
The priests do roar aloud, and round about the parents stand,
To see the sport, and with their voice do help them and their hand.

25 December
The First Day of Christmas

# FEASTING

Serving the Boar's Head

It is a holy time, a duty in Christians for the remembrance of Christ
and custom among friends for the maintenance of good fellowship.
I hold it a memory of the Heaven's love and the world's peace, the
mirth of the honest, and the meeting of the friendly.

Nicholas Breton, *Fantasticks*, 1626

hroughout Tudor England, everyone went to church on Christmas morning before tucking into the traditional good dinner. The degree to which our Tudor ancestors participated in Christmas celebrations varied depending upon whether they were rich or poor, or where they lived. Most people lived in the countryside, but for those in towns there might be a chance to see free pageants and ceremonies. In London, for example, the Worshipful Company of Butchers marched, with drummers, in a colourful street procession to present a boar's head to the Lord Mayor. The ceremony dated back to 1343, as a mark of gratitude for '... a parcel of land adjoining the Fleet (river) for the purposes of cleansing the entrails of beasts in the said water' – and it still takes place to this day. But the rule of the season, for everyone, was hospitality. People visited family, and there was as much eating and drinking as they could afford.

Christmas Day was a time for feasting, dancing, singing and watching plays, but above all, for splendid religious observances. It began with three Masses and the chanting of Christ's genealogy, as congregations held lighted tapers symbolising the coming of 'the Light of the World'. At court, there were solemn ceremonies. Henry VIII would hear Mass in his closet before going in procession to the Chapel Royal for matins, where he himself participated in the service and the choir sang 'Gloria in Excelsis'.

Everyone put on their best at Christmas, in honour of the season. At court, the King wore new clothes; royal attendants and servants were given new attire and liveries, and if they were lucky, might be granted annuities and pensions.

## Christmas dinner
*'In honour of the King of Bliss'*

A lavish Christmas dinner, served in honour of the Nativity, followed the traditional religious observances, and those who had fasted for Advent no doubt came to it with a sharpened appetite.

Plum porridge was much enjoyed as an appetiser to line the stomach before the rich dinner to come. It was a thick broth of mutton or beef, boiled in a skin with plums, spices, dried fruits, breadcrumbs and wine. In the later sixteenth century, flour was added to it to make a pudding or cake. Centuries later, the Victorians would remove the meat and turn plum porridge into the rich Christmas pudding we know today, serving it as a dessert.

An alternative to plum pudding was figgy pudding, famously demanded in the carol 'We Wish You a Merry Christmas', which itself dates from the sixteenth century. Figgy pudding had been enjoyed as a festive appetiser since medieval times, and there was a prevalent belief that Christ had eaten figs on His fateful journey to Jerusalem. There is a recipe for figgy pudding in a manuscript called The Form of Cury (now in the British Library), which was compiled by the master cook to King Richard II in 1392:

> Take almonds blanched, grind them and draw them up with water and wine: quarter figs, whole raisins. Cast powdered ginger and honey clarified, seethe [boil] it well and salt it, and serve forth.

For Christmas dinner, all classes enjoyed the seasonal favourite, brawn, which was fatty cuts of boar meat or pork, sometimes cooked in wine, and served sliced, spiced, and garnished with gilded rosemary, bay leaves, fruits, or a sprig of yew whitened with egg or flour to make it look as though it had been dusted with snow. Brawn was so popular at court that extra cooking ranges had to be built in the kitchens of Greenwich Palace for the 'seething and boiling of brawns'. The choicest cuts, the forequarters of the boar, were served to people of status, while the rest – the 'souse' – went to the servants.

The first course, however, was traditionally a boar's head. Boned, stuffed with forcemeat, smeared with mustard, dressed in herbs and fruits with a roasted apple in its mouth, and sometimes even painted bright colours, it would be ceremonially carried in, resplendent on its platter, by the steward or the head of the household, 'with the blast of trumpets and the waving of banners, with the sound of drums and pipes, so that many a heart was uplifted at the melody'. The custom continued at court until the reign of Queen Victoria.

As the wild boar gradually became extinct, its presence at the Yuletide feast was increasingly reserved for noblemen who could afford to fit out a hunting party to track down and kill the elusive beast. By Tudor times, the boar's head was a status symbol, and it was particularly associated with Queen's College, Oxford, where it had been served on the Saturday before Christmas since 1341, a tradition that continues to this day in commemoration of a medieval student who fought off a wild boar armed only with a volume of Aristotle. The King of France once sent Henry VIII a Christmas gift of boar pâté; on another occasion he sent him wild boar to hunt, as they had become so scarce in England.

As the boar's head was carried into the hall, a carol would be sung. At least four celebrating the dish survive from the fifteenth century, but the best known is 'The Boar's Head Carol', which was printed in Wynkyn de Worde's *Christmasse Carolles newley enprinted* in 1521:

The boar's head in hand bear I,
Bedeck'd with bays and rosemary,
And I pray you, my masters, be merry
*Quot estis in convivio.*
*Caput apri defero*
*Reddens laudes Domino*

[Lo, bchold the head I bring
Giving praise to God we sing]

The boar's head, as I understand,
Is the rarest dish in all this land,
Which thus bedeck'd with a gay garland
Let us *servire cantico.*
*Caput apri defero*
*Reddens laudes Domino*

Our steward hath provided this
In honour of the King of Bliss;
Which on this day to be served is
*In Reginensi atrio.*
*Caput apri defero*
*Reddens laudes Domino*

Next came a variety of rich meats, which might include larks, partridges, quails, beef, mutton, hens, capons and soused veal, all presented ceremoniously. An anonymous poem of the fifteenth century describes the kind of fare that was eaten:

Then comes in the second course with mickle [much] pride,
The cranes, the herons, the bitterns, by their side
To partridges and the plovers, the woodcocks, and the snipe.

Furmity for pottage, with venison fine,
And the umbles [entrails] of the doe and all that ever comes in,

Capons well baked, with the pieces of the roe,
Raisins of currants, with other spices mo[re].

For the poor, meat was a rare luxury. Lesser mortals usually ate pork, or whatever birds they could catch, though the better-off might enjoy poultry such as chicken or goose. Tradition has it that in 1588, Elizabeth I ordered that everyone should eat goose for Christmas dinner, as it was the first meal she had been served after the victory over the Spanish Armada, and she believed that this gesture would be a fitting tribute to the English sailors who had fought off the Spaniards. The tale is said to be the origin of people eating goose at Michaelmas, but as the Armada was won in August, it is unlikely that Elizabeth ever gave such an order; she would have known that her poorer subjects could not have obeyed it, as goose was an expensive luxury.

It is often claimed that turkey was first introduced into England by a navigator called William Strickland, who in 1550 was granted a coat of arms that featured 'a turkeycock in his pride proper'. But he was born around 1530, and there is a record of the first turkeys arriving in England from the New World in 1526, when six birds imported at Bristol sold for 2d each. There was a widespread misapprehension that turkey came from the east, via Turkey, which is why it was called a turkeycock; the French, however, thought it came from India, so they called it d'Inde (now 'dinde'). Turkey was soon prized for its flavour. It became a domestic fowl in the 1530s, was sold in markets from the 1540s, and had been added to the repertoire of popular Christmas dishes by the end of Elizabeth's reign, sometimes served instead of peacock or swan, although it would be centuries before it fully ousted them, or the traditional meats.

Stuffing, known as forcemeat and made with egg, currants, pork and herbs, is first known to have been served with poultry in 1538. Brussels sprouts are first recorded in 1587.

A dessert called frumenty was extremely popular at Christmas, and was served with meat. Recipes vary, but it was essentially a mixture of wheat boiled in milk with eggs, fruit, spices, sugar, almond milk and cream. This is the one Richard II's master cook made:

> Take clean wheat and break it well in a mortar till the holes gone off; seethe it till it breast in water. Nim [take] it up and let it cool. Take good broth and sweet milk of almond and temper it therewith. Nim yolks of eggs raw and saffron and cast thereto; salt it: let it not boil after the eggs been cast therein. Mess it forth with venison or with fat mutton fresh.

Christmas pudding was also enjoyed; in Tudor times, it was a kind of suet pudding. Several 'receipt books' survive from the period, in which housewives recorded not only recipes, but accounts, household tips, medical cures, and advice on conception and giving birth; such books were passed down the generations, and doubtless women pooled their wisdom. Elinor, the wife of Sir Richard Fettiplace of Appleton Manor, Oxfordshire, compiled her 'Receipt Book' in 1604, when she was about thirty-four; in it she included a recipe 'for a Christmas pudding':

Take twelve eggs and break them then take crumbs of bread, and mace, and currants, and dates cut small, and some ox suet small minced and some saffron, put all these in a sheep's maw [gullet] and so boil it.

A delightful tradition holds sway in London's Middle Temple Hall, of which Elizabeth I was a good patron; the Bench Table that survives at its head was her gift. So warm was the welcome of the lawyers that the Queen is said to have baked them a Christmas pudding, and in commemoration of this, a pudding was served every year, using her recipe, until 1966. In 1971, Queen Elizabeth the Queen Mother revived the tradition, stirring a new pudding for the lawyers.

Mince pies, or Christmas pies, as they were known, were made with shredded leftover meats – preferably mutton, in commemoration of the shepherds – to which suet, sugar, dried fruits and spices were added. There were supposed to be thirteen ingredients, in honour of Christ and His Apostles. Some pies were gilded. The spices and gilding harked back to the gifts of the Magi – and proclaimed the status of the host. Often a baby Jesus made of pastry would adorn the top of the pie, the pastry case being fashioned to look like a crib; such pies were called Nativity pies.

These Christmas pies were huge, unlike the small ones we eat today, and they were cut with spoons, since it was believed to be unlucky to cut them with knives. The first piece was given to the youngest person in the company, who made a wish as they ate it.

Elinor Fettiplace gives a filling for mince pies:

Parboil your mutton, then take as much suet as meat, & mince it both small, then put mace & nutmegs & cinnamon, & sugar & orange peels, & currants & great raisins, & a little rosewater, put all these to the meat, beat your spices & orange peel very small, & mingle your fruit & spice & all together, with the meat, and so bake it; put as much currants as meat & twice as much sugar as salt, put some ginger into it, let the suet be beef suet, for it is better than mutton suet.

Replete after their great Christmas dinner, the company would now proceed to enjoy the many pleasures that the season had to offer.

26 December
The Second Day of Christmas

# OFFERING

Blessing horses on Saint Stephen's Day

Then followeth Saint Stephen's Day, whereon doth every man

His horses jaunt and course abroad, as swiftly as he can.

Until they do extremely sweat, and then they let them blood,

For this being done upon this day, they say doth do them good,

And keeps them from all maladies and sickness through the year,

As if that Stephen any time took charge of horses here.

Thomas Kirchmaier, 1553

t Stephen was the patron saint of horses. On St Stephen's Day, 26 December, people in Germany and northern Europe took their beribboned horses to be blessed by the local priest, and it was believed that they should be taken out for a long ceremonial ride and then bled to ensure the continuance of their good health.

In England, on St Stephen's Day it was traditional for people to go from house to house visiting neighbours, family and friends. 'Make We Merry', an English carol dating from before 1536, might well describe such visits:

Make we merry, both more and less
For now is the time of Christëmas

Let no man come into this hall,
Groom, page nor yet marshall,

But that some sport he bring withall,
For now is the time of Christëmas.

If that he say he cannot sing,
Some other sport then let him bring,
That it may please at this feasting,
For now is the time of Christëmas.

If he say he can naught do,
Then for my love ask him no mo,
But to the stocks then let him go,
For now is the time of Christëmas.

# Charity
*'Ye who now will bless the poor'*

As described in the famous carol 'Good King Wenceslas', 'the feast of Stephen', the first Christian martyr, was traditionally the day for charity, for giving alms or leftovers to the poor. St Stephen, a devout follower of Christ, was a deacon of the early Church, whose responsibilities included succouring the poor. He was accused of blasphemy by his Jewish persecutors, but forgave them even as they stoned him to death.

It was the custom in Tudor times for the more affluent to distribute gifts, or 'boxes' containing money, to servants, apprentices, tradesmen and the needy. These, and alms boxes in churches, were opened on 26 December, which became known as Boxing Day from the seventeenth century.

Carols were written to celebrate St Stephen's Day, such as 'Aya, Martyr Stephane', dating from *c*.1425. The most famous commemorates another, later Christian martyr. The melody of 'Good King Wenceslas' originated as a spring carol of the thirteenth century; it appeared in *Piae Cantiones*, a Finnish collection of medieval Latin songs published in 1582 in Sweden. The words, however, are Victorian; they relate to Wenceslaus, Duke of Bohemia, who was assassinated in the tenth century, posthumously named a king, and subsequently made a saint. In the twelfth century, it was said of him that 'rising every night from his noble bed, with bare feet and only one chamberlain, he went around to God's churches and gave alms generously to widows, orphans, those in prison and afflicted by every difficulty, so much so that he was considered, not a prince, but the father of all the wretched'.

# Wren Day
*'Bury the wren'*

In Ireland, the Isle of Man and parts of Wales, up till around 1900, St Stephen's Day was also known as Wren Day. For hundreds of years the wren was hunted on St Stephen's Day, either in the tradition of a pagan sacrifice, or in the belief that it had betrayed St Stephen to his persecutors by singing to them of his whereabouts. Bands of 'wren boys' would attempt to catch a wren, or make a dummy one, and parade it about the town caged or nailed to a post, singing this traditional verse:

The wren, the wren, the king of all birds,
St Stephen's Day was caught in the furze,
Although he was little his honour was great,
Jump up me lads and give him a treat.
Up with the kettle and down with the pan,
And give us a penny to bury the wren.

Those who gave a penny to the boys were rewarded with one of the wren's feathers, which was said to bring them good luck.

27 December
The Third Day of Christmas

# WASSAIL

The Wassail Bowl

Good bread and good drink,
A good fire in the hall,
Brawn, pudding and souse,
And good mustard withal,
Beef, mutton and pork shred,
Pies of the best,
Pig, veal, goose and capon,
And turkey well dressed;
Cheese, apples and nuts, jolly carols to hear,
As them in the country is counted good cheer.

Thomas Tusser

enry VIII kept Christmas with 'much nobleness and open court' and 'great plenty of viands'. It was incumbent upon kings and nobles to keep open house, host great feasts and dispense hospitality throughout the twelve days, putting into practice the obligations that people of wealth and status owed to their servants and tenants and the less fortunate members of society. Observing Christmas could be a costly business, and such hospitality lightened the burden for the less well-off, ensuring that all could enjoy the season. It was also a display of the superior status and power of those doing the giving. Some kept open house from Martinmas (11 November) to Candlemas (2 February), welcoming friends and visitors and mitigating the privations of the winter months for the poor who came to receive their charity. They might entertain, in abundant fashion, up to a hundred people in their hall, twice a day, in the Christmas period.

In Henry VIII's reign, more than a thousand people dined at court at Yuletide; an Italian visitor noted that on one occasion, the guests remained at table for over seven hours. All meats were carried into the dining hall with fanfares and ceremony. There were two or three courses at every feast, each with a lavish selection of dishes. A world away from the enduring chicken-throwing image of Henry VIII popularised by Charles Laughton in the 1933 film *The Private Life of Henry VIII*, the table manners of the King and his courtiers were usually refined and decorous – apart from the time when Henry got bored and began pelting his guests with sugar plums.

## Wine

*'Good drink thereto, luscious and fine'*

The feast of St John the Evangelist, 27 December, often saw riotous carousing and feasting, for the saint was said miraculously to have recovered from drinking poisoned wine. In commemoration of St John, wine was consumed in huge quantities on his feast day, for it was believed to give men strength and women beauty – which it probably did in the eyes of those who had drunk to excess. For the common people, who were used to drinking weak ale all year, wine was a potent delight, and many would overindulge, contributing to the riotousness of the season. But society set its limits. 'Swearers and swaggerers are sent away to the ale-house, and unruly wenches go in danger of judgment.'

But the Lutheran pastor Thomas Kirchmaier saw virtue in the wine drunk on St John's Day:

> Next, John, the son of Zebedee, hath his appointed day,
> Who once, by cruel tyrant's will, constrained was, they say,
> Strong poison up to drink, therefore the Papists do believe
> That whoso puts their trust in him, no poison them can grieve.
> The wine beside that hallowed is, in worship of his name,
> The priests do give the people that bring money for the same.
> And after with the selfsame wine are little manchets [white bread
>     rolls] made,
> Against the boisterous winter storms, and sundry such like trade.
> The men upon this solemn day do take this holy wine,
> To make them strong, so do the maids to make them fair and fine.

Such English wine as was produced was of poor quality, so most wine was imported from Anjou, Gascony and Burgundy; over 120 varieties were known. It was bought by the barrel, not bottled. Regarded as a gentleman's drink, wine was expensive, and was very much a status symbol. Many sixteenth-century wines did not keep well; those that did often had a higher alcohol content than today (up to 17 per cent). Sweet, strong wines, such as Osney from Alsace, were very popular.

Most people drank ale. In Henry VIII's reign, beer imported from Flanders gained in popularity, despite the King's efforts to ban it. Neither drink was very potent, but specially brewed

Christmas ale and beer were consumed in large quantities. An anonymous fifteenth-century poet wrote of the

> Good drink thereto, luscious and fine,
> Bluet of Allemain, Romney, and wine,
> Good brewed ale and wine …

Spices and pressed apples were added to beer to make a seasonal drink known as lamb's wool, and they were also added to wine, which, when warmed, made a drink called hippocras, which we would call mulled wine. This was often served at the end of an evening of festivities. Wine was drunk young, which was why there was always a rush to import sufficient quantities for Christmas.

# Wassailing
*'Love and joy come to you'*

The Christmas custom of wassailing was enormously popular at all levels of society. The name comes from the Norse *ves heill* and the Middle English *wes heil*, meaning 'your good health', and the custom derives from an ancient fertility rite practised in the days of pagan tree worship. The wooden wassail bowl, decorated with ribbons, contained hot ale, beer or cider, apples, sugar, spices, rosemary and a crust of bread at the bottom. People would pass the bowl, crying, 'Wassail!' and each recipient would take a drink and pass it on, saying, 'Drinkhail!' The crust of bread at the bottom of the wassail bowl was reserved for the most important person in the room, the origin of the later custom of 'toasting' at celebrations.

Often, children would carry the wassail bowl from house to house, with seasonal greetings and blessings, to be shared and replenished, hopefully generously, as Thomas Kirchmaier describes:

> There cities are where boys and girls together still do run
> About the streets with like as soon as night begins to come,
> And bring abroad their wassail-bowls, who well rewarded be
> With cakes, and cheese, and great good cheer, and money
>     plenteously.

On Twelfth Night, farmers would wassail their trees by pouring the drink over the roots to ensure a bountiful harvest. The practice survives even today in the West Country, and, of course, it was commemorated by Herrick:

> Wassail the trees, that they may bear
> You many a plum and many a pear:
> For more or less fruits they will bring,
> As you do give them wassailing.

The famous carol 'Here We Come A-Wassailing' is often said to date from the nineteenth century, but a version of it was known in the early seventeenth century, and included a verse that portrayed the reality of life for many children at Christmas, which shows why wassailing was so popular:

Good master and mistress,
While you're sitting by the fire,
Pray think of us poor children,
Who are wandering in the mire.

# Feasting

*'At Christmas we banquet'*

Christmas was a time not only for drinking to excess, but for eating too. Kings, queens and all ranks of their subjects feasted and revelled their way through the festive season, free for a short time from everyday cares. After the Advent fast, the rich fare of Christmas must have been eagerly anticipated, especially by the poor who waited at the gates of great houses for the leftovers that were traditionally sent down to them. 'A good fire heats all the house,' it was said, 'and a full alms-basket makes the beggar's prayers.'

As wild boars were dying out in England, domesticated boars were fattened up from September onwards. November saw the beginning of the slaughter of livestock that would provide meat for the winter; when not eaten fresh, it was preserved by salting, sousing, brawning, pickling or smoking. Christmas fell in a hunting season, which meant that fresh game for the table was plentiful. A lot of poaching went on; one wit wrote: 'Stolen venison is sweet, and a fat coney [rabbit] is worth money: pitfalls are now set for small birds, and a woodcock hangs himself in a gin.' As Yuletide approached, 'the beasts, fowl, and fish come to a general execution, and the corn is ground to dust for the bakehouse and the pastry'.

At Christmas, all Tudor kitchens were working at full stretch. In the royal palaces, the cooks toiled over vast ovens, roaring fires, and charcoal stoves; kitchens were hot, smoky and noisy, and frequently resembled 'veritable hells'. The average Tudor kitchen was a large room with workbenches, a table and possibly a stone sink. Food was stowed in barrels or earthenware pots. Water had to be obtained from a well or a stream, and cooking was done over an open fire in – or on – the hearth. Every aspect of food preparation, from cooking to preserving to brewing, was done in the kitchen.

The staple dish of a Tudor Christmas was meat. Even if Christmas Day fell on a Friday or religious fast day, when people were supposed to abstain from eating meat, the Church permitted meat to be eaten instead of fish, although there was no such dispensation for New Year's Day. At Christmas dinner at Ingatestone Hall in 1551, Sir William Petre and his family and guests ate six boiled and six roast joints of beef, a neck of mutton, a loin of pork, a breast of pork, a goose and four coneys. For supper, five more joints of mutton, a neck of pork, two coneys, a woodcock and a venison pasty were served.

'The peacock in his pride' (peacocks were symbolic of vanity and pride) and roast swan were high-status birds and therefore popular Christmas fare at court. Royalty and the very rich might be served a 'cockatrice', which comprised the roasted forequarters of a pig with the hindquarters of a capon. Such high-status poultry was often served in its plumage, with gold leaf gilding its beak and coloured beads inserted for eyes. The birds had to be carefully skinned, with the feathered skin being reserved to wrap around the cooked carcass. To the sound of trumpeters blowing on silver horns, the reconstructed peacock or swan, on a gold or silver platter, would be carried in procession and presented at the high table. At a royal Christmas feast in 1500, 104 peacocks were served.

Sometimes, warden (pear) pies, containing pears spiced with cloves, mace, cinnamon and ginger, and sprinkled with sugar, were served at Christmas dinner. Eight were served to Sir William Petre's household in 1551. In Shakespeare's *A Winter's Tale*, Perdita makes a festive warden pie:

> Let me see; what am I to buy? Three pound of sugar, five pound of currants, rice ... I must have saffron to colour the warden pies; mace; dates? – none, that's out of my note; nutmegs, seven; a race or two of ginger, but that I may beg; four pound of prunes, and as many raisins o' th' sun.

In *A book of cookery. Very necessary for all such as delight therein*, compiled by 'A.W.' and dating from 1591, we find instructions on 'How to bake Wardens':

> Core your wardens and pare them, and parboil them and lay them in your paste, and put in every warden where you take out the core a

64

clove or twain, put to them sugar, ginger, cinnamon, more cinnamon than ginger, make your crust very fine and somewhat thick, and bake them leisurely.

At court and in great households, twenty sorts of jellies in the shape of castles or animals might be served for dessert. The *pièce de résistance* was a 'subtlety' – which sounds like a misnomer, for there was little that was subtle in fantastic sugar sculptures carved in the forms of castles, coats of arms, ships or some other noble design, painted and gilded, and served with a flourish to the high table. But the word 'subtle' then meant 'clever' or 'skilled', and making subtleties required a high degree of dexterity and artistry on the part of the confectioner, for they were constructed entirely of sugar and almond paste, and could be two or three feet high and intricately detailed. Subtleties might have looked amazing, but, unsurprisingly, they were 'an assault for valiant teeth'. Henry VIII had a sweet tooth. He even appointed a woman (one of only two in his employ) to make his puddings. Her name was Mrs Cornwallis, and her confections so delighted the King that he rewarded her with a fine house in Aldgate.

Sometimes, the dessert course, or 'void', would be served as a private banquet in the King or Queen's privy chamber, or in one of the exquisite little banqueting houses in the palace gardens. Here, sweetmeats – what we would call canapés – were served buffet style, with the guests helping themselves after the servants had been dismissed. Among the delicacies were suckets (pieces of fruit in syrup, which were eaten with forklike sucket spoons), marzipan treats, marchpane, jellies, biscuits, sweets called 'kissing comfits' (or muscadines) made of sugar fondant and nuts, mounds of syllabub called 'Spanish paps [nipples]', and apples with caraway seeds and sugared spices. Some of these sweetmeats were known aphrodisiacs. All were passed round on glass or silver stands, or ornate spice plates; Henry VIII had one of silver gilt set upon four antique heads with an elaborate cover of silver, agate, porcelain, and emerald chased with roses and fleurs-de-lis.

Only the most privileged were invited to the void, for the sugar and spices used to make the comfits and sweetmeats were costly. Marchpane was a favourite, being a kind of almond shortbread made with rose water, iced, or gilded with gold leaf, and sometimes decorated with comfits.

At the end of the evening, the King and Queen were ceremonially presented with their gold cups, and hippocras and wafers were served before the company departed, some no doubt – if the aphrodisiacs had done their work – to their amorous beds.

28 December
The Fourth Day of Christmas

MISRULE

The Lord of Misrule

Then comes the day that calls to mind the cruel Herod's strife,
Who seeking Christ to kill, the King of everlasting life,
Destroyed all the infants young, a beast unmerciless,
And put to death all such as were of two years age or less.
To them the sinful wretches cry and earnestly do pray
To get them pardon for their faults, and wipe their sins away.

Thomas Kirchmaier, 1553

he feast of the Holy Innocents on 28 December commemorates a paranoid King Herod ordering the slaying of all infant boys under two years of age, in an attempt to destroy the infant Christ – the Massacre of the Innocents – and for that reason was called Childermas. Due to its sombre associations, it was a day of fasting for adults, and sometimes, when children woke up, they were whipped – perhaps not too hard – as they lay in bed, to remind them of the suffering of the murdered innocents. However, for the rest of the day, they were allowed greater licence and even permitted to play in church. It was, essentially, a children's feast.

It was believed that bad luck would come to those who worked on Childermas, and that the day of the week on which it fell would be unlucky for the rest of the year.

The famous, and desolate, 'Coventry Carol', from *The Pageant of the Shearmen and Tailors* in the Coventry cycle of mystery plays (which are described in the 2 January chapter), tells the story of the Massacre of the Innocents from the point of view of three mothers of Bethlehem. The words date from 1534, but the music comes from a manuscript of the pageant written in 1591. The play had been suppressed by then due to the Reformation, but the carol had survived.

Lully, lulla, thou little tiny child,
Bye bye, lully, lullay, thou little tiny child,
Bye bye, lully, lullay!

O sisters two, how may we do
For to preserve this day
This poor youngling for whom we do sing
Bye bye, lully, lullay?

Herod the King, in his raging,
Charged he hath this day
His men of might in his own sight
All young children to slay!

And woe is me, poor child, for thee,
And ever mourn and may
For thy parting neither say nor sing,
Bye bye, lully, lullay.

# Lords of Misrule and other fools in fancy dress

### 'Lusty guts'

There was in the King's house, wherever he was lodged, a Lord
of Misrule, and the like had ye in the house of every nobleman of
honour or good worship, were he temporal or spiritual.

John Stow, *The Survey of London*, 1598

Throughout Britain, the Christmas period was a time for liberty,
relaxation and subverting the rules. One element of the Roman
festival of Saturnalia that had survived was that of role reversal
among the hierarchical ranks of society, and between the sexes.
For a few days, rank took second place to revelry, social barriers
came tumbling down, and restraint was set aside. At the same
time, festive licence served to underline the normal roles of those
who participated: no one forgot who was master and who was
servant. In Scotland, the twelve days of Christmas were called
the 'Daft Days'.

In great households, these twelve days of feasting, banqueting,
pageantry and convivial merrymaking were presided over not
by the King or the master of the household, but by the Lord of
Misrule, or 'Master of Merry Disports', who acted as master
of ceremonies and took charge of the Christmas revelry. These
Lords of Misrule were paid handsomely for their services.

Philip Stubbs, a disapproving Puritan, has left an evocative description of Elizabethan Lords of Misrule.

All the wild [hot]heads of the parish choose them a grand captain, whom they ennoble with the title of my Lord of Misrule, and then they crown him with great solemnity. This king, anointed, chooseth forth twenty, forty, three-score or a hundred lusty guts like himself to wait upon his lordly majesty and to guard his noble person. They bedeck themselves with scarves, ribbons and laces, hanged all over with gold rings, precious stones and other jewels; this done, they tie about either leg twenty or forty bells, with rich handkerchiefs in their hands, borrowed for the most part of their pretty mopsies from bussing [kissing] them in the dark. Then have they their hobby horses, dragons and other antiques, together with their bawdy pipers and thundering drummers.

The train of a Lord of Misrule might include heralds, magicians, and fools in fancy dress. Some even had a mock gibbet so that they could send anyone who disobeyed them to be 'executed'.

Lords of Misrule were at their most popular in the fifteenth century and in early Tudor England. The Lord Mayor of London, local sheriffs, cities, towns and parishes all had their own Lords of Misrule, 'ever contending, without quarrel or offence, who should make the rarest pastimes to delight the beholders', for the company had to be kept entertained. 'The Lord of Misrule is no mean man for his time, and the guests of the high table must lack no wine: the lusty bloods must look about them like men, and piping and dancing puts away much melancholy.'

Even the monarch had to obey the commands of the Lord of Misrule. Will Wynesbury was Lord of Misrule in the first year of Henry VIII's reign, and impudently asked his sovereign for £5 towards his expenses. 'If it shall like Your Grace to give me too much,' he added mischievously, 'I will give you none again, and if Your Grace give me too little, I will ask more!' Henry was greatly amused.

The seasonal role reversal extended to the Church also. Prior to the Dissolution of the Monasteries in the 1530s, Abbots of Misrule held sway in abbeys and priories, just as Lords of Misrule did in secular households. Following medieval custom, 'boy bishops' replaced adult prelates, and were allowed the same privileges as Lords of Misrule. Appointed on St Nicholas's Day, 6 December, and allowed to hold office until Holy Innocents' Day, they were chosen from cathedral choirs – often the longest-serving chorister was selected – and invested with costly miniature vestments, mitres and croziers, purpose-made and beautifully worked.

During their term of office, they were deferred to as if they were real bishops, enjoyed actual episcopal power, and took all the services the adult bishop would have taken, apart from Mass. When they preached sermons, they were given gifts in reward. They could appoint cathedral canons from their chorister friends, and if they died in office, they would be buried with the full honours of a real bishop; the tombstone of one, in episcopal robes, can be seen in Salisbury Cathedral. But there were many complaints that boy bishops carried out their duties mischievously and without due respect, and that, when they and their 'clergy' went begging for alms at houses around the towns, they practised what amounted to extortion. Many people must have exhaled in relief when the boy bishops' rule came to an end on Holy Innocents' Day. Nevertheless, these disorderly little prelates could create havoc in the last hours before sober normality returned, since they were protected by a law that forbade anyone to disrupt their services or throw things at them.

Henry VIII himself appointed a boy bishop from his choristers, the Children of the Chapel Royal, to take the place of his senior chaplain, and he once rewarded a lad called Nicholas with 10 marks – equivalent to £3,570 today – for taking this role.

Another example of inverted roles was the seasonal custom of 'barring out' schoolmasters, which originated in Tudor times. Boys would stockpile provisions, as if for a siege, and barricade the school doors. Indignant masters would sometimes use force to get in, and fights and floggings might even ensue. Usually the teacher was allowed to enter on condition that he administered fewer beatings and permitted more holidays. The custom flourished until the nineteenth century, chiefly in northern England, Scotland and Ireland.

# Father Christmas

*'Make good cheer and be right merry'*

In the train of the Lord of Misrule, there was sometimes a character called 'Captain Christmas' or 'Prince Christmas', whose role was to ensure that everyone made merry at Yuletide.

By Tudor times, the tradition of Christmas being personified by one person, like Father Christmas or Santa Claus today, was well established. In fact, it was centuries old. The Saxons had welcomed in winter in the guise of King Winter, or King Frost, or Father Time, giving him a crown and an honoured place by the hearth, in the hope that he would be kind to them. Norse tradition had it that at Yule, the god Woden, the lord of magic and healing, came down to earth on his eight-legged horse called Sleipnir, joined gatherings by the fire, and left gifts of bread and much goodwill; in return, offerings were left out for him. He was even known as 'Yule-Father'. The Christian saint Nicholas, Bishop of Myra, is said to have dropped a sack of coins down the chimney of some poor girls who, lacking dowries, were about to resort to prostitution. He later became the patron saint of children, and his cult was very popular. All these elements would be present in the much later figure of Father Christmas.

Dating from the late fifteenth century, the carol 'Sir Christëmas' embodied the medieval personification of the season, which had certainly been established by 1400:

'Nowell, nowell, nowell, nowell.'
'Who is there that singeth so nowell, nowell, nowell?'

'I am here, Sir Christëmas.'
'Welcome, my lord Sir Christëmas,
Welcome to us all, both more and less,
Come near, nowell.'
'Dieus wous garde, bewe sieurs, tidings I you bring:
A maid hath borne a child full young,
The which causeth (you) for to sing,
Nowell.'

'Christ is now born of a pure maid,
In an ox-stall he is laid,
Whereof sing we alle at a brayde,
Nowell.'

'Bevvex bien par tutte la company,
Make good cheer and be right merry,
And sing with us now joyfully,
Nowell.'

A favourite character in the mumming plays that were so popular in medieval and Tudor times was actually called Father Christmas, Old Christmas or Old Man Winter. Clad in green, and wearing a grotesque mask and a wig, he would rampage about, shouting and brandishing a great club – unlike Santa today! This Father Christmas was bent on exhorting his audience to behave themselves, and to maintain the old customs of Yuletide:

Here comes I, Old Father Christmas;
Welcome or welcome not,
I hope Old Father Christmas
Will never be forgot.
[A pause.]
Who went to the orchard to steal apples to make gooseberry pies
against Christmas?

In 1616, the playwright Ben Jonson appeared in his own *Christmas, His Masque*, playing 'Christmas, old Christmas, Christmas of London, and Captain Christmas', wearing ordinary 'round hose, long stockings, a close doublet, a high crown'd hat with a brooch, a long thin beard, a truncheon, little ruffs, white shoes, his scarfs, and garters tied across, and his drum beaten before him'. This recalls the mummers' Father Christmas, but the club has been replaced by a truncheon.

Jonson's Father Christmas had ten children, whose names – as we mentioned in our introduction – reflected the various aspects of Yuletide: Misrule, Carol, Mince-Pie, Gambol, Post and Pair, New Year's Gift, Mumming, Wassail, Offering and Baby-Cake, the last being named in honour of the miniature versions of the Twelfth Night cake that were sometimes served. These 'children' wore outlandish costumes, with New Year's Gift entering 'in a blue coat (serving-man like) with an orange, and a sprig of rosemary on his head, his hat full of brooches, with a collar of gingerbread, his torch-bearer carrying a marchpane, with a bottle of wine on either arm'. They dance, and old Father Christmas cries, 'Well done, boys, my fine boys, my bully boys!'

29 December
The Fifth Day of Christmas

# GAMBOL

When the Thames froze at Christmas, people sported on it;
later, there were 'frost fairs' on the ice

Till sleep takes place of weariness.
And thus throughout, with Christmas plays,
Frolic the full twelve holy-days.

Robert Herrick, 'A New Year's Gift to Sir Simeon Steward', 1628

he Fifth Day of Christmas – 29 December – was the anniversary of the martyrdom of Archbishop Thomas Becket in 1170 in Canterbury Cathedral, the tragic climax to a long dispute between Becket and Henry II. St Thomas was one of the most popular saints in England, and many people would have marked his feast day by making a pilgrimage along the Pilgrims' Way made famous by Geoffrey Chaucer in *The Canterbury Tales* to Becket's glittering, bejewelled shrine at Canterbury, which was visited by up to 100,000 people a year. In turn, they would place their hands inside the apertures in the side of the shrine, to get as close as possible to the saint's relics, and pray for healing and miracles. Then they might buy a souvenir, perhaps a pilgrim badge depicting St Thomas.

# Revelry and Sports

*'Frolic the full twelve holy-days'*

For those not away on pilgrimage, Christmas continued to be a season of revelry and 'honest pastimes'. The court was always full, and the public were often allowed in to watch the 'goodly and gorgeous mummeries [the word meant both merrymaking and mummers' plays]' – usually from a safe distance – and to partake of the festive fare on offer. Pageants, masques, interludes, plays and music, devised under the direction of the Master of the Revels, carried on throughout the twelve days of Christmas. At Christmas 1526, Henry VIII had his ten-year-old daughter, the Princess Mary, brought to court, and there were 'great plenty of victuals, revels, masques, disguisings, banquets and jousts'. The King led the Princess out before the company, and an anonymous poet among those watching captured the moment in verse: 'I saw a king and a princess dancing before my face, more like a god and a goddess …'

The fourteenth-century poem 'Sir Gawain and the Green Knight' describes the medieval idyll of Christmas, which was still current in Tudor England: 'King Arthur lay at Camelot upon a Christmas-tide, with many a gallant lord and lovely lady, and they made rich revel and mirth, and were free from care.' They held tournaments, then returned to court to sing carols. 'And the feasting was with all the meat and mirth men could devise, and glorious to hear was the noisy glee by day and the dancing by night; and all was joyous in hall and chamber.'

Christmas was also a time for hunting, sport and outdoor pastimes. John Stow recalled that, in his youth in the reign of Henry VII, a quintain – a post with a sandbag suspended from it – had been set up in Cornhill so that the citizens could have 'merry disports' in tilting at it with lances. When the Thames froze over in 1564, people played football on the ice 'as boldly as if it had been on dry land', many courtiers 'shot daily at pricks [targets]' set up on the frozen water, and 'both men and women went daily on the Thames in greater number than in any street of London' until the ice began to thaw on 3 January. In 1608, the river froze over again, and 'certain youths burnt a gallon of wine upon the ice, and made all the passengers partakers', while one 'honest woman had a great longing to have her husband get her with child upon the Thames'.

In 1509, at Richmond, Henry VIII celebrated his first Christmas as king with jousting before the palace gates, on what is now Richmond Green, where 'many notable feats of arms were proved'. At Christmas 1524, he took part in his last major tournament, which was to have formed part of a magnificent pageant, 'The Castle of Loyalty'. A castle twenty feet square and fifty feet high was built to his design in the tiltyard at Greenwich, 'but the carpenters were so dull they understood not his intent, and wrought all thing contrary'. One can imagine the royal complaints, as the structure was evidently not stable enough to withstand an assault and the pageant had to be abandoned, although the jousts went ahead. They began with the Queen, Katherine of Aragon, seating herself in the flimsily built castle; there then came before her two 'ancient knights' who 'craved her leave to break spears'. When Katherine praised their courage in performing feats of chivalry at their advanced age, they threw off their disguises to reveal the thirty-four-year-old King and his friend, the Duke of Suffolk.

30 December
The Sixth Day of Christmas

# CAROL

The Town Waits singing carols

It is now Christmas, and not a cup of drink must pass without a carol.

Nicholas Breton, *Fantasticks*, 1626

# Nowell, Nowell

*'At Christmas, of Christ many carols we sing'*

Our most popular Christmas carols today date from Victorian times, although many have their origins in the more distant past, for the practice of carol-singing dates back many centuries. Many so-called Victorian carols are based on early ones. Besides giving the world a whole new canon of carols, the Victorians often used old tunes that would have been known in Tudor times, and harmonised them, sometimes adding new words. 'The First Nowell' and 'God Rest You Merry, Gentlemen' ('The London Carol') are both thought to date from the sixteenth century. The tune of 'While Shepherds Watched Their Flocks' was written by Christopher Tye (1505–72), choirmaster at Ely Cathedral and musical adviser to Edward VI, although the words are seventeenth-century.

In Tudor England, music was an integral part of the Christmas festivities, when 'musicians now make their instruments speak out, and a good song is worth the hearing'. The Tudor monarchs were all passionate about music, which was seen as a necessary adjunct to royal magnificence. Under Henry VIII, English music progressed from the formal medieval style to one more florid and versatile, and most early Tudor music was polyphonic, having many voices or sounds. Sacred music now reached new heights of grandeur and artistic intricacy in the hands of a few gifted composers under royal patronage, while secular music was growing in popularity. Traditional ballads were much enjoyed; Henry himself composed them. It was during his reign, in 1530, that the first book of music was printed in England, by Wynkyn de Worde; it contains various secular part-songs.

Making music was an essential accomplishment for the nobility and gentry, some of whom were competent composers, players or singers, and many nobles employed their own bands of musicians, who performed in the minstrels' galleries above their dining halls.

Even so, early-sixteenth-century music was less sophisticated than that of later centuries. Few instruments survive, and sheet music is poorly annotated, so modern musicians have to 'realise' each piece on reconstructed instruments, which sometimes involves guesswork, especially in regard to percussion. Instruments were not as finely tuned as now, and modern scales not developed until later in the century.

The best-loved songs of the Christmas season were, of course, carols: popular devotional songs often written in the vernacular with a smattering of Latin. Originally round dances with lively rhythms, they were sung and danced at many feasts of the Church, including Easter, and especially at Christmas, when they were performed around the cribs in churches. The proliferation of organ books in the sixteenth century, and parish records of organ repairs, show that hymns and carols were sung in services with accompaniment. Most carols are anonymous, their words and music having been passed down as an oral tradition through the generations, which is why it is sometimes impossible to date their origin.

Often, carols would be sung by groups of singers called the town waits, who were appointed by the civic authorities to provide music for ceremonial occasions, often out of doors. The waits also tramped the night streets, singing for the pleasure of householders and hoping to be given food or money in exchange, much as carol singers do today.

The first carols in English were translated or composed by Franciscan friars in the thirteenth century as aids to learning about the Scriptures. One of the most enduring of these is 'Angelus ad Virginem', which dates from *c*.1250 and is mentioned by Chaucer in 'The Miller's Tale'. The earliest surviving carols by English composers date from the fifteenth century, a period in which the carol gained hugely in regard, as witnessed by the volume of surviving texts and settings. One of the most favoured was the 'Cherry Tree Carol', also known as 'Joseph Was an Old Man'; another was 'Adam Lay Ybounden'. People in Tudor times would have known many of these older carols, and possibly others dating back centuries.

The majority of carols focused on the Nativity, and were songs of celebration and rejoicing, such as 'Make We Joy' and 'Alleluia, Now May We Well Mirthes Make', both from *c.*1450; others featured pagan elements such as holly, ivy and the boar's head. The words 'alleluia' and 'nowell' were used liberally. There is a delightful everyday realism in the way the infant Christ and His Mother are portrayed as natural, living mortals with whom ordinary people could identify. It is the Three Kings who appear as distant, magnificent figures, in contrast to the humble baby lying in the manger. This tender realism is particularly evident in the fifteenth-century carols 'There Is No Rose of Such Virtue', 'I Sing of a Maiden' and 'Lullay My Liking' (the original tune of which is unknown):

Lullay my liking,
My dear Son, my Sweeting;
Lullay my dear Heart,
Mine own dear Darling.

I saw a fair maiden
Sitten and sing:
She lulled a little child,
A sweet Lording
Lullay my liking ...

There was mickle melody
At that child's birth:
Though the songsters were heavenly

96

They made mickle mirth.
Lullay my liking …
Angels bright they sang that night
And said unto that Child
'Blessed be Thou and so be she
That is so meek and mild.'
Lullay my liking …

Pray we now to that child,
As to His Mother dear,
God grant them all His blessing
That now maken cheer.
Lullay my liking …

It can also be seen in the 'Lute Book Lullaby' ('Sweet Was the Song the Virgin Sang') from William Ballet's *Lute Book* of 1590, now in Trinity College, Dublin:

Lalula, lalula, lalulaby, sweet babe, sang she,
And rocked Him sweetly on her knee.

Some carols that are still sung, in one form or another, by choirs in the twenty-first century originated in medieval Germany, and may well have been known in England before the Tudor era. 'In Dulci Jubilo', 'Personent Hodie' and 'Quem Pastores' date from the fourteenth century, and 'Es is ein Ros' entsprungen' (better known from the nineteenth century as 'A Great and Mighty Wonder') from the fifteenth, with music composed by the great

German composer Michael Praetorius (1571–1621). An English translation of 'In Dulci Jubilo' appeared in John Wedderburn's lost *Good and Godly Ballads* (1540); it is known today in its magnificent harmonised form by J. S. Bach, but the tune is the same.

Some famous carols, such as 'Ding Dong Merrily on High' – originally a dance called the 'Branle de l'Officiel' (the words are nineteenth-century) – were printed in Thoinot Arbeau's collection of dance tunes, *Orchésographie*, in 1589 in France. More of the carols we know today had appeared in *Piae Cantiones* in 1582, notably 'Up Good Christen Folk and Listen'.

Several English carols survive from Tudor times. A few – including 'The Salutation Carol', 'In Bethlehem, that Fair City' and 'The Seven Joys of Mary' – appear in the commonplace book of Richard Hill, a London grocer, compiled between 1504 and 1536 (now in Balliol College, Oxford). Wynkyn de Worde's *Christmasse Carolles*, published in 1521, is the earliest recorded printed collection, although only one leaf of it, with two carols, survives, in the Bodleian Library. Another collection, put together by Richard Kele, appeared around 1550.

Among very early Tudor carols were 'The Golden Carol' of *c.*1490, and 'Sir Christëmas', which appears in the Ritson Manuscript in the British Library, a collection of English and Latin songs and music compiled between the time of Edward IV (1461–83) and 1510.

'As I Outrode This Endris Night' is a less-well-known carol from *The Pageant of the Shearmen and Tailors*, from which 'The Coventry Carol' comes, and was added to it in 1591.

As I outrode this endris [recently past] night
Of three jolly shepherds I saw a sight;
And all about their fold a star shone bright.
They sang terly terlow.
So merrily the shepherds their pipes can blow.

Down from Heaven so high of angels
There came a great company with joy and mirth.
And great solemnity.
They sang terly terlow.
So merrily the shepherds their pipes can blow.

In 1535, 'Von Himmel Hoch', a Christmas Eve carol that the founder of the Protestant religion, Martin Luther, had written for his son Hans, was published in Germany. It was certainly sung in Scotland, where a translation was printed in 1567 as 'Ane Song of the Birth of Christ', so it was probably sung in England too. Today, it is better known as 'Balulalow':

O my deir hairt, young Jesus sweit
Prepare Thy cradle in my spreit,
And I sall rock Thee in my hairt
And never mair fra Thee depart;

But I sall praise Thee evermore
With sangis sweit unto Thy gloir!
The knees of my hairt sall I bow
And sing Thy praise, balulalow.

Around 1600, the great Elizabethan dramatist Ben Jonson composed 'An Hymn on the Nativity of My Saviour'.

I sing the birth was born to-night,
The author both of life and light;
The angels so did sound it.
And like the ravish'd shepherds said,
Who saw the light, and were afraid,
Yet search'd, and true they found it.

The Son of God, th' eternal King,
That did us all salvation bring,
And freed the soul from danger;
He whom the whole world could not take,
The Word, which heaven and earth did make,
Was now laid in a manger.

What comfort by him do we win,
Who made himself the price of sin,
To make us heirs of glory!
To see this babe, all innocence;
A martyr born in our defence:
Can man forget the story?

In Tudor times, the gentlemen and children of the Chapel Royal would come before the monarch and sing carols, for which they would be rewarded with gifts of money. In 1502, Elizabeth of York, queen of Henry VII, rewarded William Cornish, later Master of the Children and Choristers of the Chapel Royal, with 4s. 4d for 'setting of a carol upon Christmas Day'. At the court of her son, Henry VIII, carols were sung and danced 'to the great rejoicing of the Queen and the nobles'.

Sacred music at court was the province of the highly trained, elite choir of the Chapel Royal, which 'gloriously' sang Mass daily and performed regularly for the King, especially when he wished to impress guests. Their voices, wrote an Italian visitor, 'are really rather divine than human. They did not chant, but sang like angels.' Most of the music sung by the Chapel Royal was composed by its talented members, among them the accomplished organist and composer William Byrd, Gentleman of the Chapel Royal under Queen Elizabeth, and often called 'the father of English music'. For Christmas, he composed a carol-motet, 'Out of the Orient Crystal Skies' (or 'Falan-tidings', as it became known, after its unique refrain in the last line), for a soprano and four viols. It is one of the finest musical pieces of the English Renaissance.

Out of the orient, crystal skies
A blazing star did shine,
Showing the place where poorly lies
A blessed Babe divine.
Born of a maid of royal blood
Who Mary hight by name,
A sacred rose which once did bud
By grace of heavenly flame.

This shining star three kings did guide
Even from the furthest East,
To Bethlehem where it betide
This blessed Babe did rest,

Laid in a silly manger poor,
Betwixt an ox and ass,
Whom these three kings did all adore
As God's high pleasure was.
And for the joy of His great birth
A thousand angels sing:
'Glory and peace unto the earth
Where born is this new King!'

The shepherds dwelling thee about,
Where they this news did know,
Came singing all even in a rout,
Falantidingdido, falantidingdido, falantidingdido!

In the 1580s, William Byrd was a frequent Christmas guest of the Petre family at Ingatestone Hall, and took with him musicians who were paid £3 by the steward to play the viols.

31 December
The Seventh Day of Christmas

# POST AND PAIR

Hoodman Blind

Of Christmas sports, the wassail-bowl,
That toss'd up, after Fox-i'-th'-hole;
Of Blind-man-buff, and of the care
That young men have to Shoe the Mare;

Robert Herrick, 'A New Year's Gift to Sir Simeon Steward', 1628

# Games

*'Christmas sports'*

Although there is no record from the sixteenth century of people gathering on New Year's Eve to see the old year out and welcome in the new one at midnight, and most of the old customs associated with New Year's Eve (such as first-footing) do not pre-date the nineteenth century, the day was still one for revelry. Traditionally, the seventh day was the occasion for games and sporting competitions.

Christmas celebrations in Tudor times could be very boisterous. For the rich, they included hunting and outdoor sports, but sport was heavily controlled by the government, and was a rarity in the lives of people whose waking hours were filled with relentless manual work. In 1542, determined to maintain England's military strength and its fearsome reputation for winning battles through the skill of its archers, Henry VIII passed a law banning all sports on Christmas Day except archery. He also enacted that artificers, husbandmen, labourers, mariners, fishermen, watermen, craftsmen, servants and apprentices could play cards, dice, football, bowls, tennis, quoits, ninepins and shove groat only at Christmas. Small wonder that people threw themselves into the revelry with gusto, and that there were complaints that 'cards and dice purge many a purse'.

The better-off played board games such as chess or backgammon. Guessing games, word games, dice and cards, at which huge sums might be won or lost, were widely enjoyed. Favourite card games – and there were many – included primero, which originated in Spain or Italy; mumchance, which had to be played in silence; click-clack; imperial, a form of piquet; trump, an early version of whist; noddy, which would evolve into cribbage; post and pair, which was similar to primero; and slam, a lively discarding game. In laugh and lie down, which dates from before 1522, players still in the game were meant to laugh when others were 'out'. Gleek is described in *The Church of the Evil Men and Women* (1522), probably because it was a devious game of trickery. On New Year's Day 1587, Robert Dudley, Earl of Leicester, played a card game called double-hand lodum, in which the loser won. In January 1530, Henry VIII lost the staggering sums of £100 playing cards with the gentlemen of his Privy Chamber and £450 at dominoes.

Henry also enjoyed the aristocratic game of shovelboard, skimming metal discs or coins along extended narrow tables to see which landed furthest away. Ordinary mortals played another version, shove groat (later shove ha'penny), in taverns. Billiards was popular, as was troll-my-dame, in which balls were rolled through hoops; Shakespeare mentions it in *A Winter's Tale*. At court, all games were organised by the Knight Marshal of the Household; elsewhere, by the Lord of Misrule.

Parlour games, as later generations called them, were widely enjoyed at Christmas. Among the best known was hide-and-seek, which is believed to have originated in second-century Greece. Shakespeare refers to it twice. In *Love's Labour's Lost* (1598), Biron says, 'All hid, all hid; an old infant play'; and Hamlet alludes to the game when he says, 'Hide Fox, and all after.'

A variant of hide-and-seek was called by-your-leave; in 1572, Richard Huloet's *Dictionarie* described it as 'a play that children have, where one sitting blindfold in the middle, bideth so till the rest have hidden themselves, and then he going to seek them; if any get his place in the mean space, that same is king in his room'.

The boisterous, and sometimes rough, hoodman blind (later known as blind man's buff, 'buff' meaning buffet) was widely played, and so called because, in the Middle Ages, people turned their hoods back to front, or pulled them forward over their eyes, then chased the other players until they caught one. That person became the next hoodman. By Tudor times, blindfolds were used. When Hamlet asks his mother how she could have consented to wed his uncle, Claudius, he says: 'What devil was't that thus hath cozen'd you at hoodman-blind?'

In the sixteenth-century game fox in the hole, one player was chosen as the fox, and it was his or her task to catch the other players, who were all designated chickens. Once caught, they were consigned to the fox's den. The chicken who eluded the fox longer than the rest took his place in the next round.

Shoe the mare, an Elizabethan game, was for robust boys and young men. 'The youth show their agility in shoeing of the wild mare.' A beam – 'the mare' – was suspended from the ceiling, strong and high enough for a man to sit astride it with his legs dangling. Using a hammer, he had to give the underside of the beam thirty-two blows without falling off. Inevitably this game caused much competitiveness among the men. It is the basis of the nursery rhyme:

> Shoe the colt,
> Shoe the wild mare;
> Here a nail,
> There a nail,
> Yet she goes bare.

One mid-sixteenth-century game, hot cockles, verged on the licentious. A blindfolded player groped for one of those sitting around, placed his or her head in their lap, and raised a hand, palm upwards, behind him. The person on whom he was lying slapped it, and he had to guess who it was.

The most hazardous game was snap-dragon (or flap-dragon), which originated in Tudor times and was a favourite on Christmas Eve. Raisins, almonds, currants or candied fruits were placed in a bowl of warm brandy, which was then ignited, and the players had to snatch the fruit without burning their fingers. This may be the origin of the custom of pouring brandy on the Christmas pudding and lighting it. In *Love's Labour's Lost*, Shakespeare has the bumpkin Costard say to Moth, 'Thou art easier swallowed than a flap-dragon.' It is not recommended that readers try this game at home.

Prisoner's base, or barres, was a boisterous game dating from the fourteenth century, in which each team tried to capture members of the other and hold them prisoner in a designated place. Another Tudor Christmas game was dun in the mire, which required a player to lift, or 'rescue', a heavy log representing a horse and carry it away in the face of other players trying to stop him, or make him drop it on the toes of the guests. The game was known to Chaucer in the fourteenth century, and Shakespeare refers to it in *Romeo and Juliet* – 'If thou art dun, we'll draw thee from the mire.'

At court and in great houses, there would be shuttlecock, skittles, fortune-telling, music, dancing and paid entertainers such as acrobats, tumblers and fire-eaters, as well as the jokes and antics of jesters, and much tomfoolery:

Come follow, follow me,
Those that good fellows be,
   Into the buttery
   Our manhood for to try;
The master keeps a bounteous house,
And gives leave freely to carouse.
When we have done this fray,
Then we will go to play
   At cards or else at dice,
   And be rich in a trice.

And when that's spent the day
We'll Christmas gambols play,
    At hot cockles beside
    And then go to all-hide,
With many other pretty toys,
Men, women, youths, maids, girls and boys.


Come, let's dance round the hall,
And let's for liquor call;
    Put apples in the fire,
    Sweet maids, I you desire;
And let a bowl be spiced well
Of happy stuff that doth excel.

1 January

The Eighth Day of Christmas

# NEW YEAR'S GIFT

A couple of capons

The old year now away is fled,
The new year it is entered;
Then let us all our sins down tread,
    And joyfully all appear.
Let's merry be this holiday,
And let us run with sport and play,
Hang sorrow, let's cast care away
    God send us a merry new year!

And now with New-Year's gifts each friend
Unto each other they do send;
God grant we may our lives amend,
    And that truth may now appear.
Now like the snake cast off your skin
Of evil thoughts and wicked sin,
And to amend this new year begin:
    God send us a merry new year!

And now let all the company
In friendly manner all agree,
For we are here welcome all may see
    Unto this jolly good cheer.
I thank my master and my dame,
The which are founders of the same,
To eat, to drink now is no shame:
    God send us a happy new year!

Come lads and lasses every one,

Jack, Tom, Dick, Bess, Mary and Joan,

Let's cut the meat unto the bone,

  For welcome you need not fear.

And here for good liquor you shall not lack,

It will whet my brains and strengthen my back;

This jolly good cheer it must go to wrack:

  God send us a happy new year!


Come, give's more liquor when I do call,

I'll drink to each one in this hall,

I hope that so loud I must not bawl,

  So unto me lend an ear.

Good fortune to my master send,

And to our dame which is our friend,

Lord bless us all, and so I end:

  God send us a happy new year!

Traditional, 'The Old Year Now Away Is Fled'*

*      First printed 1642, and sung to the tune of 'Greensleeves', which dates from
1580, when it was called 'A New Northern Ditty of ye Lady Greensleeves'.

n Tudor times, the Julian calendar (first implemented by Julius Caesar in 46 BC) was observed. The liturgical new year began on 1 January, which was known as New Year's Day, but the date did not change on documents until 25 March, Lady Day, or the feast of the Annunciation, on which the legal year officially began. It was on the feast of the Annunciation that Mary was told she would be the mother of Jesus. In 1582, in Catholic countries, the Julian calendar was replaced by the Gregorian calendar when Pope Gregory XIII recognised 1 January as New Year's Day for both religious and secular purposes. However, European Protestants reacted with suspicion to the Papal bull, and Britain would stick to the old style until 1752.

According to the Bible, 1 January fell eight days after the birth of Jesus, and on this day, His mother's feast day, He was named and circumcised. Observation of the two feasts became popular in the late fifteenth century, and a Mass in honour of the Virgin Mary was often celebrated.

New Year's Day was a very special occasion. Kings and queens always wore their crowns and their royal robes furred with ermine, and went in procession to chapel, and afterwards they held court before presiding over a great feast. They and their special guests would then retire to a private chamber or banqueting house for a banquet.

## Gifts

*'And now with New-Year's gifts*
*each friend unto each other they do send'*

The most important aspect of New Year's Day was the presents. The giving of gifts had been a feature of the Roman Saturnalia, and the custom had survived into the Tudor age, when presents were exchanged not on Christmas Day, but on New Year's Day. In feudal times, it had been customary for peasants, and in fact all who owed allegiance to an overlord, to give him a present at New Year.

Gift-giving was a popular custom, as Thomas Kirchmaier described:

The next to this is New-Year's Day, whereon to every friend

They costly presents in do bring and New-Year's gifts do send.
These gifts the husband gives his wife, and father eke the child,
And master on his men bestows the like, with favour mild,
And good beginning of the year they wish and wish again,
According to the ancient guise of heathen people vain.

But although the giving of gifts was widespread among the upper and middle classes, there are no records of the custom being observed in the homes of poor people at this time. Middle-class people might 'send a couple of capons or any other presents to a friend in the twelve days', perhaps oranges stuck with cloves, gloves, money or pins. Lovers sometimes exchanged nutmegs glazed with egg-white to spice their drinks.

At the Tudor court, Henry VIII and Elizabeth I encouraged the practice of present-giving, and it was expected that every courtier and servant would give the monarch a gift. Queen Elizabeth even decreed the amount each person was to spend, according to their rank. Archbishops were expected to spend £40 and peers £20.

In the early Tudor period, New Year gifts were exchanged formally in the bedchambers of the King and Queen, who received them while seated on benches at the end of their beds. It is clear from Queen Elizabeth of York's privy purse expenses that she gave rewards to those lords and servants who brought her New Year's gifts, and that those payments were carefully graded according to rank, though they were 'not as good as those of the King'. Later that day, (bounty) was proclaimed in the great hall, where Henry VII and his Queen distributed gifts to members of their households.

Under the later Tudors, each gift was handed to the sovereign by the donor (or his representative) in the course of a long ceremony in the presence chamber, where the gifts – which might be gold or silver plate, jewellery or money (although Elizabeth I liked to receive costly items of clothing too) – were afterwards displayed on sideboards or trestle tables for all to see. Great lords vied with one another to give the most valuable or novel items: Cardinal Wolsey regularly gave his master the King a gold cup worth £100.

When, on New Year's Day 1538, Master John Husee came to court to deliver Lord Lisle's gifts, he found Henry VIII leaning against a cupboard as the courtiers came forward in turn with their offerings. Beside Henry stood Thomas, Lord Cromwell; Edward Seymour, Earl of Hertford (brother of the late Queen Jane); and, at the other end of the cupboard, Bryan Tuke, Henry's secretary, who was recording the gifts on a scroll.

When he saw Husee, the King seemed genuinely pleased. He smiled warmly as the gift was presented, and seemed to take longer than usual to express his thanks, enquiring about the health and activities of Lord and Lady Lisle. Among the King's gifts on display, Husee saw a clock fashioned like a book, paintings, velvet purses full of coins, costly carpets, coffers, dog collars, embroidered shirts, hawks' hoods, a gold trencher, six cheeses from Suffolk, and even a marmoset.

One gift that was undoubtedly treasured by Henry VIII was Hans Holbein's superb portrait of the two-year-old Prince Edward, wearing a wide-brimmed bonnet and clutching a gold rattle, which was given to the King on New Year's Day 1540. A delighted Henry gave Holbein a silver-gilt-covered cup made by his goldsmith, Cornelius Heyss.

Gifts presented at court to Elizabeth I included jewels and purses of gold from great nobles and officers of state, embroidered petticoats or sleeves from ladies of the bedchamber, 'a fair pair of quinces' from the Serjeant of the Pastry, a chessboard made of marchpane from the Master Cook, and boxes of sweetmeats and crystallised fruits from the Clerk of the Spicery.

Gift-giving at court was of great political significance. If the King or Queen accepted your gift you were evidently in favour, but if they rejected it, things were not looking good. In 1532, after he had separated from Katherine of Aragon, whom he was determined to divorce, Henry VIII accepted gifts from his sweetheart, Anne Boleyn, but rejected those that Katherine sent him, commanding her not to send him any in future, for he was not her lawful husband, as she should have known. In 1571, the Duke of Norfolk, while imprisoned in the Tower of London, sent Queen Elizabeth a very lavish jewel as a New Year's gift. It was rejected, and the Duke was later executed.

The New Year's gift could also be a means of regaining royal favour. In 1580, the scholarly courtier, poet and diplomat Sir Philip Sidney displeased the Queen by daring to suggest that she should not get married; but after he presented her with a jewelled whip to demonstrate his subjection to her will, she quickly forgave him.

The Tudor monarchs also gave gifts, usually items of plate, such as cups and bowls chased with the royal cipher, each weighted according to rank. Every person at court, even the most menial members of the royal household, got something. In one year, 1511, Henry VIII spent over £800 (over £400,000 today) on New Year's presents.

Henry VIII's New Year's presents reflect the complicated course of his love life. In 1510, his first New Year gift to Katherine of Aragon was a beautifully illuminated missal. In 1532, Anne Boleyn gave Henry 'darts of Biscayan fashion, richly ornamented', and in return he presented her with 'a room hung with cloth of gold and silver and crimson satin with rich embroideries'. He also gave Anne's sister, his former mistress, Mary Boleyn, a shirt with a collar of black-work embroidery. Anne's gift to him at New Year 1534 was an exquisite table fountain of gold, studded with rubies, diamonds and pearls, from which 'issueth water at the teats of three naked women standing at the foot of the fountain'; it was probably designed by Hans Holbein. At New Year 1541, the King lavished gifts on his new young wife, Katherine Howard, including two pendants each containing 26 table diamonds, another with 27 diamonds, 158 'fair pearls', a rope of 200 large pearls, and 26 clusters of pearls. On 3 January, his divorced wife, Anne of Cleves, arrived at court, bringing with her two superb horses caparisoned in purple velvet for the King and Queen. Among the gifts that Henry's daughter, the future Mary I, received in 1544 were handkerchiefs, embroidered gloves and sleeves, smocks, cushion covers, brooches, books, an inkstand and sweetmeats.

# Revelry
*'Merry, merry boys'*

New Year's Day was observed with lavish feasting and revelry. Thomas Kirchmaier, for one, looked askance at the excesses of the season:

> These eight days no man doth require his debts of any man,
> Their tables do they furnish out with all the meat they can:
> With marchpanes, tarts and custards great they drink with staring
>     eyes,
> They rout and revel, feed and feast as merry all as pies,
> As if they should at the entrance of this New Year have to die,
> Yet would they have their bellies full and ancient friends ally.

The merriment was such that New Year's Day was sometimes called the Feast of Fools. In Scotland, Twelfth Night itself was known as Unhalieday, or Unholyday. It was another occasion on which roles might be reversed and much buffoonery ensued. Parents ceded authority to their children, and in monasteries, before the Reformation, the most junior monk or nun was allowed to be abbot or abbess for the day, with mayhem ensuing. The Church tried to limit the excesses of the Feast of Fools, but with little success.

New Year's Night was the occasion for more revelry and entertainment. In 1512, at court, a pageant called 'The Fortress Dangerous' was performed. It featured a castle with towers and a dungeon, 'garnished with artillery and weapons, after the most warlike fashion', inside which were six ladies wearing gowns of russet satin 'laid all over with leaves of gold'. The castle was assaulted by the King with five other knights, and predictably the ladies, 'seeing them so lusty and courageous', readily yielded, and came down to dance with them.

At New Year, in Babylon and ancient Rome, it had been the custom to make promises to the gods to repay debts and live good lives in the year to come. For Christians, New Year was a time for reflecting on your conduct in the past year and resolving to do better in the months ahead. In medieval times, around New Year, a knight would make a 'vow of the peacock [or pheasant]', placing his hand on the roasted bird in all its finery and renewing his vow of chivalry. Thus evolved the modern secular tradition of making New Year's resolutions. It was already well established by 1667, when the celebrated diarist Samuel Pepys wrote on New Year's Eve: 'I have newly taken a solemn oath about abstaining from plays and wine, which I am resolved to keep according to the letter of the oath which I keep by me.' Within three weeks, he had broken it.

2 January

The Ninth Day of Christmas

# MUMMING

*Saint George and the Dragon*, a popular Christmas play

The play's the thing.

William Shakespeare, *Hamlet*

# Drama

*'Come, sit down, every mother's son, and rehearse your parts'*

The earliest Nativity plays in England were part of the ritual of the Church at the festival of Christmas. Performed in churchyards, streets or marketplaces, they were acted by monks, with a young girl playing the Virgin Mary.

Throughout the Middle Ages, at Christmas and great festivals, the Church had put on plays, chanted or spoken in Latin, as additions to services, for the enjoyment and edification of the people. Later, the craft and trade guilds mounted miracle or 'mystery' plays, the word mystery deriving from the Latin *misterium*, meaning a craft, trade or occupation. These too were based on stories from the Bible, of which the most popular was the Nativity, and every aspect of it, from the Annunciation to the Massacre of the Innocents, was part of the repertoire. The plays were performed on scaffolds or pageant wagons with three tiers: the action took place on the main stage, with a platform representing Heaven above, and a space for Hell below. Audiences particularly loved devils and demons, parts that offered marvellous opportunities for action, slapstick, comedy and improvisation.

Similar plays were performed by troupes of travelling actors in marketplaces and later in the courtyards of inns, where the audience watched from galleries. The George at Southwark (rebuilt in 1676) is the most famous of such inns to survive, but the oldest is the New Inn at Gloucester, dating from 1430–50. In early Tudor England, the universities of Oxford and Cambridge paid travelling players to perform during their Christmas festivities.

By the late fifteenth century, certain cycles of mystery plays had become established or famous, such as the York, Wakefield, Coventry and Chester collections. Some were performed on the feast of Corpus Christi in June, others at Christmas. These plays continued to be performed after the Reformation, but the authorities kept watch for anything contentious, and references to the Pope, the saints and the sacraments were often edited out. In the end, most mystery plays were banned, despite the protests of the merchant community for whom they had been a lucrative enterprise. The York mystery plays, performed on the feast of Corpus Christi since 1376, and the Chester plays died out in Elizabeth's reign when their texts were taken for examination by the Church and never returned.

The Coventry cycle of plays, dating from 1392, and watched by Henry VII in 1492, were suppressed in 1579, although one by the guild of smiths was performed in 1584. Most mystery plays did not survive the 1570s, and many texts are lost. Those from York, Chester and Wakefield are still in existence, thanks to being preserved by the Church, but only two of the Coventry plays survive: *The Pageant of the Shearmen and Tailors*, based on St Luke's account of the Nativity up to the Massacre of the Innocents; and *The Weavers' Play*, which continues the story with the Purification of the Blessed Virgin Mary, the Presentation of Christ in the Temple, and Christ and the Doctors.

For ordinary people in Tudor times, Christmas afforded the chance to see a mummers' play, a tradition that went all the way back to the pre-Christian era. The word 'mummers' means masked actors, for these wandering groups of often tattered amateurs always wore disguises and were not supposed to be recognised – bad luck would come to anyone who discovered their identity. They performed traditional folk plays during Yuletide gatherings, from which originated many elements of today's pantomime, such as stage fights, coarse humour, fantastical creatures, gender role reversal, and good defeating evil: Beelzebub (the Devil) was an especially popular character. Traditionally, on Christmas Eve, travelling mummers would arrive at a royal palace, great house, town or village, and perform their most popular play, which depicted St George and the Dragon, who was usually a comical character. Audiences loved the mock battles in which these old protagonists took part, and the fact that whoever was injured or slain was always restored by a doctor, death and resurrection being a traditional theme in mummers' plays. There would often be a fair maiden bearing mistletoe, and a boy carrying a wassail bowl.

Mummers expected to be paid for the entertainment they provided. 'The maskers and the mummers make the merry sport, but if they lose their money their drum goes dead.' They would also be welcomed into private houses to play cards and dice, for which they were rewarded with cakes and ale. The diarist Henry Machyn recorded that, in December 1555, he and his neighbours were guests at a great feast prepared by a Mistress Lentall of Henley-on-Thames, during which masked mummers entered singing and were afterwards invited to partake of the marmalade, gingerbread, fruit, jelly and other good things that were set out for the company.

In London, Bristol and Chester, it was forbidden to walk about masked during the twelve days of Christmas, because when masked mummers performed outdoors in darkness, there were many opportunities for crime to flourish.

In the sixteenth century, it became a tradition for entertainments to be staged on Twelfth Night, 5 January, although they were enjoyed on the other days of Christmas too. Disguisings and pageants were popular at court in the early Tudor period. Interludes – short plays deriving from late-medieval morality plays depicting the conflict between the personifications of virtue and vice – were put on at court as edifying entertainments during banquets or as diversions between the acts of dramas. Always they had a moral. The best-known example is *Everyman*, a late-fifteenth-century morality play that used allegory to show audiences how to achieve Heaven. At Christmas 1515, the Chapel Royal performed a comedy, *Troilus*

*and Pandarus,* in the great hall at Eltham Palace.

In 1510, when Henry VIII spent his first Twelfth Night as king at Westminster Palace, he and a band of noblemen put on a 'disguising'. They 'came suddenly in a morning into the Queen's chamber, all apparelled in short coats of Kentish Kendal, with hoods on their heads, and bows and arrows, like outlaws or Robin Hood's men, whereof the Queen and the ladies were abashed, as well for the strange sight, as also for their sudden coming'; but when musicians struck up a tune, they entered into the spirit of the occasion and danced with the 'outlaws'. Predictably, when the masks were removed, Robin Hood turned out to be the young King himself, 'and after dances and pastime made, they departed. Later at dinner the King arranged the seating and joked with all', and had four of his friends 'parade in strange costumes before they brought in actors to stage a play'.

In 1514, the King's new mistress, Elizabeth ('Bessie') Blount, featured prominently in a Christmas pageant at Greenwich. She and other ladies dressed up as ladies of Savoy in blue velvet gowns, gold caps, and masks, and were rescued from danger by four gallant 'Portuguese' knights, played by the King and other gentlemen. The unsuspecting Katherine of Aragon was so delighted with their 'strange apparel' that, before they all removed their masks, she invited them to dance again for her in her bedchamber. The King partnered Elizabeth Blount, and there was much laughter when the identities of the dancers were revealed. Katherine thanked the King for 'her goodly pastime, and kissed him'. Possibly Katherine got wind of her husband's affair, because on Twelfth Night 1515, when the same pageant was staged once again by popular demand, Elizabeth Blount did not take part.

In 1516, at Greenwich Palace, there was a pageant entitled 'The Garden of Esperance', which featured an entire artificial garden on a cart known as a 'pageant car'. But already pageants were losing favour in the wake of a new form of courtly entertainment.

For Twelfth Night 1511, William Cornish, the Master of the Children and Choristers of the Chapel Royal, who was responsible for the great court revels of Henry VIII's early reign, had devised something novel:

> The King with eleven other were disguised after the manner of Italy, called a masque, a thing not seen afore in England. They were apparelled in garments wrought with gold, with visors and caps of gold; and after the banquet [was] done, these masquers came in with six gentlemen, disguised in silk, bearing torches, and desired the ladies to dance. Some were content, and some that knew the fashion of it refused because it was not a thing commonly seen. After they danced and communed together, and as the fashion of the masque is, they took their leave and departed, and so did the Queen and her ladies.

What was remarkable about this masque was that rather than dancing with ladies with whom they had rehearsed, as in a pageant, the men chose their partners from the audience.

Masques, or 'masks', as they became known in England, were a form of drama in which the plot took second place to disguises, poetry, music and dancing, and they were usually performed by courtiers. Utilising spectacular costumes, scenery and effects, they began with an impressive entry, continued with a 'presentation' that often lauded the high-ranking persons watching, and ended with a dance that was frequently complicated and required skill and agility. Like pageants, many masques had allegorical or political themes. In 1517, at Eltham Palace, Henry VIII and Katherine of Aragon watched a masque entitled *Troilus and Cryseide*, which was based on the Greek myth retold as an epic poem in Middle English by Geoffrey Chaucer.

Henry VIII's growing preference for masques, in which he could show off his talents to perfection, meant that they soon replaced pageants as the court's chief form of dramatic spectacle. They were often performed at the court of Elizabeth I, and were frequently staged on New Year's Day or Twelfth Night. These were magnificent occasions, with gorgeously dressed lords and ladies mingling with players in fantastic costumes in halls lit by torches and candles. At Christmas 1572, a masque called *The Play of Narcissus* was performed at Whitehall Palace before the Queen, and featured dogs chasing a fox around the stage. The court masque reached its apogee in the Stuart court of the early seventeenth century, with magnificent productions costing the equivalent of over £1 million in today's money.

Like her father, Henry VIII, Elizabeth kept Christmas with great ceremony and splendour. Above all, she loved theatrical entertainments. But the play performed on Christmas Night 1559, early in her reign, was too salacious for the royal taste, so masquers were summoned to dance for her instead.

Thanks to the popularity of the seasonal masque, and the patronage of companies of actors by Elizabethan noblemen, Twelfth Night became a traditional time for going to the theatre. The first playhouse opened in 1576 at Shoreditch, its design being based on a galleried inn, and by the end of the century about 15,000 Londoners – possibly one fifth of the City's population – were attending the theatres every week, with takings soaring over the Christmas period.

It was often cheaper to call for a company of actors to perform a play before the court than it was to put on an entertainment, so the Queen's Men, or William Shakespeare and his associates in the Lord Chamberlain's Men, were frequently summoned to Elizabeth's court. Tradition has it that Shakespeare's *Love's Labour's Lost* was the play that was performed at Christmas 1592 before the Queen at Hampton Court by the Earl of Pembroke's Men, although it is now thought that the play dates from the mid 1590s.

At Christmas 1594, Christopher Marlowe's plays *Doctor Faustus* and *Tamburlaine the Great* were playing to packed houses at the Rose Theatre. On Christmas Day itself, a now lost play, *The Grecian Comedy*, was performed, and on St Stephen's Day, a drama called *The Siege of London*, set during the Wars of the Roses. The theatre's big hit the following Christmas was Thomas Heywood's *The Wonder of a Woman*, while in 1596 *Nebuchadnezzar* won the plaudits on Christmas Day.

Drama was hugely popular at court, where the productions could be spectacular. Shortly before Christmas 1600, Elizabeth I commissioned Shakespeare to write the comedy *Twelfth Night* as an entertainment for her guest, Virginio Orsini, Duke of Bracciano. It was to be performed at the close of the festive season at Whitehall Palace, where Elizabeth often kept Christmas. The Queen commanded that it 'be best furnished with rich apparel, have great variety and changes of music and dances, and of a subject that may be most pleasing to her Majesty'. The play expanded on the musical interludes and riotous disorder expected of the occasion – 'If music be the food of love, play on' – and featured the gender and status reversal typical of Twelfth Night, and the merriment, misrule and disguisings that prevailed.

*Twelfth Night* was probably the play that was performed on the evening of Twelfth Night 1601, when, as Orsini wrote to his wife, the Queen commanded him

> to go along, discoursing with her. Her Majesty mounted the stairs, amid such sounding of trumpets that methought I was on the field of war, and entered a public hall, where all around were rising steps with ladies and divers consorts of music. As soon as her Majesty was set in her place, many ladies and knights began a grand ball. When this came to an end, there was a mingled comedy, with pieces of music and dances. Her Majesty conversed continually with me, and when the comedy was finished, I waited upon her to her lodgings.

Sadly for us, Orsini – who was the model for Shakespeare's 'noble Duke, in nature as in name' – saved the details of the comedy to relate to his wife in person.

When the first Stuart King, James I, wanted to see a play performed at court one Christmas night, and was told by his new

English courtiers that it was not the fashion, he snapped that he would make it one. Soon, plays were being performed at court on every night of the twelve days, with a fabulous masque upon Twelfth Night. In 1604, Sir Dudley Carleton wrote to a friend:

The first holy days we had every night a public play in the great hall, at which the King was ever present and liked or disliked as he saw cause, but it seems he takes an extraordinary pleasure in them. The Queen [Anne of Denmark] and Prince [Henry] were more the players' friends, for on other nights they had them privately and have since taken them to their protection. On New Year's night we had a play of Robin Goodfellow [a variant of A Midsummer Night's Dream] and a masque brought in by a magician of China. There was a heaven built at the lower end of the hall out of which our magician came down, and thereupon a traverse was drawn [to reveal] masquers sitting in a vaulty place with their torchbearers and other lights, which was no unpleasing spectacle. The Sunday following was the great day of the Queen's mask. The one end [of the hall] was made into a rock, and in several places the Waits placed, in attire like savages, loose mantles and petticoats of different colours, the stuffs embroidered satins and cloth of gold and silver, for the which they were beholden to Queen Elizabeth's wardrobe. So ended that night's sport with the end of our Christmas gambols.

# 3 January
## The Tenth Day of Christmas

# OLD CHRISTMAS
# IS UNDONE

Stripping the churches of Catholic images

Good news from heaven the angels bring,

Glad tidings to the earth they sing:

To us this day a child is given,

To crown us with the joy of heaven.

Martin Luther, extracted from the *Lutheran Church Book**


… keeping Christ's birthday as you are wont to do.


John Calvin, 1551


*        Text based on Luke 2:1–18.

# Reformation

*'Cursed then are all enjoyments'*

On 3 January 1526, the fabulously wealthy and powerful Cardinal Wolsey hosted a feast that was unexpectedly interrupted by a burst of cannon-fire from outside. This heralded the arrival of a troupe of visitors wearing disguises. Invited to guess which one was the King, the Cardinal incorrectly identified Sir Edward Neville as his sovereign, much to the amusement of Henry and everyone else. Nothing discomfited, Wolsey arranged for his new guests to be seated at table and, astonishing those already present, who had eaten to satiety, signalled for another two hundred dishes to be brought to table, 'to the great comfort of the King'.

Only five years later, the great Cardinal would be disgraced and dead, England would be on course for the Reformation, and the old beliefs would be questioned.

Until the early seventeenth century, the English Christmas was celebrated much as it had been in the Middle Ages, and retained the character of a medieval festival, but after Henry VIII broke with Rome and made himself Supreme Head of the Church of England in 1534, everything the Church had ever taught was questioned. Christmas was seen by some reformers as pagan in origin and little more than an excuse for merriment. Separating themselves from Roman Catholic practices, Protestant leaders were critical of the many feast days of the Catholic Church and the superstitious veneration of saints. Christmas became a point of contention among many Protestants, although Martin Luther, father of the Reformation, permitted the celebration of certain feast days, including Christmas. Luther remained attached to the marking of Christ's Nativity in the life of the Church, and he was not alone.

The influential hard-line Swiss reformer, John Calvin, sought to reclaim Christmas as a celebration of Christ's Nativity and to purge the excesses traditionally associated with both the feast and what he viewed as the 'abomination' of the Mass. Certainly the Reformation witnessed the removal of saints' days and various traditional feasts, but most reformed Protestants of the sixteenth century continued to celebrate Christmas and Easter, marking the birth, death and resurrection of Jesus Christ.

A very notable exception was John Knox, a Scottish follower of Calvin and one of the driving forces behind the Scottish Reformation of 1560. Knox wanted to worship only when specifically commanded in the Bible, not on the date of the Roman Saturnalia. He – and the Puritans after him – pointed out that nowhere in the Scriptures was there any command or justification to celebrate the birth of Christ, especially on 25 December, for there was no evidence that Christ had been born on that date. They deplored the fact that the medieval Church had christianised pagan celebrations such as the winter solstice and Saturnalia.

In the Scottish Reformation, clear stands against Christmas were taken by the Kirk (the established church of Scotland) in 1560 and 1566, before the festival was abolished in 1583, reinstated by James VI, and banned again in 1640. 'The Kirk within this kingdom is now purged of all superstitious observation of days.' Christmas Day would not be a holiday again until 1958, and Boxing Day not until 1974. The New Year's Eve festivity, Hogmanay, was by far the largest celebration in Scotland.

The Reformation in England largely embraced Christmas, its impact so slight as to be hard to discern. Henry VIII banned boy bishops in 1542, because they mocked the ecclesiastical authority that was now invested in him. But the practice continued, only to be suppressed by Archbishop Thomas Cranmer, who regarded it as part of the mummery and superstition of the medieval Church. Queen Mary revoked the ban and tried to revive the tradition, but with the accession of Elizabeth, it lapsed in many areas, although it survived in some cathedrals. Some other old customs, such as that of children leading prayers on Holy Innocents' Day at Godstow Abbey in Oxfordshire, were also banned by Henry VIII.

Carol-singing declined after the Reformation, despite Martin Luther and other reformers encouraging the use of carols in worship. The mandatory Advent fast was no longer observed, as it was now perceived as a Papist practice. The Reformed Church believed that a Christian might choose to fast as a spiritual exercise to discipline his own flesh, but that the time and manner of fasting should be left to the individual's discretion.

Nevertheless, Christmas rituals continued much as before – until the reign of Henry VIII's son, Edward VI, who ruled from 1547 till 1553. His reign did not witness any significant changes in the secular aspects of Christmas, but it had an impact on many of the religious rituals.

Edward VI was raised by Protestant reformers with strong views against Catholicism. This boy King was to be identified with Josiah, an Old Testament king who suppressed idolatry, and his reformers took a harsh line. In 1550, Parliament ordered that all images should be removed from churches, and in 1552 the Act of Uniformity eliminated any vestiges of the old faith. Across the country, a wave of mass iconoclasm was unleashed, with medieval wall paintings whitewashed and stained glass destroyed, while images of saints were removed or defaced.

The cult of the Virgin Mary was abolished. Reformers recognised Mary as the Mother of God, but felt that she should not be worshipped in the same way as Christ; therefore, paintings and statues of her were destroyed. Christmas cribs and Nativity scenes began to disappear, and images of angels – key participants in the Christmas story – were also removed. For Catholics, the first Mass on Christmas Day was the 'Angels' Mass', but for the evangelical reformers, flying angels were worse than unnecessary – they were blasphemous.

The lighting of candles other than for illumination was

banned. This would have had a dramatic impact on Christmas church services, as virtually all pre-Reformation churchwardens' accounts record that candles were made, or bought in bulk, for Christmas morning. Churches that were once ablaze with light, to reflect the glory of God, were now lit only with dim lamps. Some pre-Reformation accounts make special mention of lighting the rood loft, the carved wooden balcony fixed above the screen that divided nave from chancel, and laity from clergy. Its principal feature, the rood – a large effigy of the crucified Christ – also disappeared from English churches at this time.

Finally, and most importantly, those used to hearing a Christmas Mass – which meant virtually everyone – would now be listening to a service conducted in English from the *Book of Common Prayer*, written by Archbishop Thomas Cranmer and published in January 1549. This was now the only legal form of service in England, having replaced the banned Catholic Latin liturgy.

Some legislation from Edward's reign is surprising. In 1551, a law was passed that everybody had to walk to church on Christmas Day, as opposed to riding; technically this is still law today. In the mid 1550s, the Church banned all pictures of the baby Jesus having a bath. It had been common for years for artists to paint Jesus having His first bath, but the Church stated that He was so pure that He did not need one – hence it was illegal to paint a picture of Jesus being bathed by Mary and Joseph.

With so many rituals of the old Roman Mass stripped away, and holy days abolished, it is a wonder that Christmas continued in Reformation England; but the simple reason for its survival was its widespread popularity at all levels of society. Edward VI enjoyed all the traditional pleasures of the season, and delighted in entertainments. After all, this was the boy King who, aged nine, stopped his coronation procession to watch a Spanish acrobat performing on a wire near the old St Paul's Cathedral.

King Edward kept a full open table at Christmas and particularly enjoyed Twelfth Night revels, which reached a peak of extravagance under his chief adviser, John Dudley, Duke of Northumberland (Lord President of the Council from 1550–3), who was keen to keep his young master entertained. The revels of 1551/2 were particularly elaborate and magnificent, costing over £500, with the King himself recording the schedule of entertainments for Twelfth Night in his journal.

The boy King died before his sixteenth birthday, in 1553, and was succeeded by his Catholic half-sister, Mary I. Her re-establishment of the 'old religion' would have been apparent in the Marian Christmas, with a return to the Latin liturgy, candles, rood screens, angels and cribs. But these practices would not long outlive her, because early in the reign of her half-sister, Elizabeth I, who ruled from 1558 to 1603, England again turned officially Protestant.

The Elizabethan festive season was as colourful as any earlier Tudor Christmas; Elizabeth's religious settlement was a hybrid of Protestant liturgy and Catholic traditions, particularly in church music. But during her reign, life for her poorer subjects, who had lived through a quarter-century of Reformation and Counter-Reformation, became increasingly hard. Disastrous harvests between 1594 and 1597 doubled the price of wheat. The religious houses, which would have dispensed some charity to the destitute, particularly at Christmas, had long been closed. By the 1590s, few among the poor could indulge in the customary feasts and treats of the celebrated twelve days. At the same time, a tiny social elite enjoyed a period of unrivalled brilliance at court in literature and music. If ordinary people were scaling down their Christmas celebrations, it was for economic reasons, and not because of the Reformation.

The real attack on Christmas in England would come in the next century. It would prove to be sustained, fierce and hugely divisive, but ultimately, Christmas would survive.

4 January
The Eleventh Day of Christmas

MINCE-PIE

Christmas is banned

There shall be no more cakes and ale.

William Shakespeare, *Twelfth Night*

# Puritans

*'The superstitious time of the Nativity'*

In 1632, the Puritan lawyer William Prynne wondered why people could not observe Christmas without 'drinking, roaring, healthing, dicing, carding, masques and staging plays, which better become the sacrifices of Bacchus than the incarnation of our most blessed Saviour'.

Increasingly in the late sixteenth and early seventeenth centuries, Puritans – strict 'pure' Protestants – came to frown upon the celebration of Christmas as an unwelcome survival of the Roman Catholic faith. They disliked what they saw as the waste, extravagance, disorder, sin and immorality of the season. More importantly, they saw Christmas – Christ's Mass – as a Popish festival with no biblical justification, and called it by a variety of derogatory names, such as 'the old heathen's feasting day', 'the profane man's ranting day' or 'the superstitious man's idol day'. It should, they thought, be 'the true Christian man's fasting day'. Philip Stubbs, a stout Puritan pamphleteer, deplored the custom of appointing Lords of Misrule, and accused them of striking up 'the Devil's dance' and going in rowdy procession to church 'like devils incarnate'.

In Shakespeare's *Twelfth Night*, Malvolio is accused of being a Puritan, and is humiliated and punished accordingly, to which his final, prescient riposte is: 'I'll be revenged on the whole pack of you!'

In 1616, in the satirical *Christmas, his Masque*, the playwright Ben Jonson had several digs at Puritan attempts to stop 'old Christmas' hosting the revelry:

Why Gentlemen, do you know what you do? Ha! Would you ha' kept me out? Christmas, old Christmas? Christmas of London, and Captain Christmas? Pray you let me be brought before my Lord Chamberlain, I'll not be answer'd else. 'Tis merry in hall when beards wag all: I ha' seen the time you ha' wish'd for me, for a merry Christmas, and now you ha' me; they would not let me in! I must come another time! A good jest, as if I could come more than once a year; why, I am no dangerous person, and so I told my friends o' the Guard. I am old Gregory Christmas still, and though I come out of Popes-Head Alley, as good a Protestant as any i' my parish!

Christmas at court, however, continued to be observed with all the customary magnificence and ever more fantastic and colourful entertainments. James I, who succeeded Elizabeth I in 1603 and established the Stuart dynasty in England, had decided views on how the season should be celebrated. His own book, *Basilikon Doran*, suggested that holy days such as Christmas ought to be marked by 'honest games' and merriment. He openly deplored the Calvinist Scottish Kirk's ban on Christmas, and wrote: 'Certain days in the year should be appointed for delighting the people, for convening of neighbours, for entertaining friendship and heartliness, by honest feasting and merriness.'

Writing in the 1640s, Richard Carpenter, a Protestant convert, observed that the recusant Catholic gentry were noted for their 'great Christmases', although many English Protestants viewed Christmas festivities as the trappings of popery, anti-Christian 'rags of the Beast'. They also thought that the lavish overindulgence of King Charles I and his Queen, Henrietta Maria, went beyond the limits of morality. It was one of many complaints that contributed to the clash between Crown and Parliament – and ultimately, from 1642, the descent of the three kingdoms of the British Isles into a bloody and divisive civil war.

It is a common myth that Oliver Cromwell himself 'banned' Christmas; it was the elected Parliament that took the initiative, in 1644–7, with his approval, in passing a series of Acts criminalising the celebration, along with other saints' and holy days. It was asserted that 'more mischief is that time committed than in all the year besides, what masking and mumming, whereby robbery, whoredom, murder and what-not; what dicing and carding, what eating and drinking, what banqueting and feasting is then used, to the great dishonour of God and impoverishing of the realm'. Instead, 'Christ-tide' should be kept, if at all, merely as a day of fasting and seeking the Lord, 'with the more solemn humiliation because it may call to remembrance our sins and the sins of our forefathers, who have turned this feast, pretending the memory of Christ, into an extreme forgetfulness of Him'.

It was decreed that 'The observation of Christmas having been deemed a sacrilege, the exchange of gifts and greetings, dressing in fine clothings, feasting and similar satanical practices, are hereby FORBIDDEN, with the offender liable to a fine of five shillings.' There were to be no carols and 'no prayers or sermons in the churches on 25 December, and whosoever shall hang at his door any rosemary, holly or bays, or other superstitious herb, shall be liable to the penalties decreed by ordinance; and whosoever shall make, or cause to be made, either plum pudding or Nativity pies, is hereby warned that it is contrary to the said ordinance'. Parliament also ordered that shops and markets were to stay open for business on 25 December. Anyone caught breaking the law was liable to a fine or imprisonment.

From Oxford, the wartime capital of Charles I, the Royalist satirist John Taylor lamented in his pamphlet *The Complaint of Christmas*, 'thus are the merry lords of misrule suppressed by the mad lords of bad rule at Westminster'. Taylor was a Thames waterman turned poet, who shows us how an ordinary person might have enjoyed Christmas in the early Stuart period. He writes of dancing, singing carols, telling stories, playing cards and games such as 'hot cockles', prior to the government bans.

On 24 December 1644, the editor of a pro-Parliamentarian news pamphlet expressed his support for the MPs' decision to favour the monthly fast over the traditional feast, but admitted that 'the Parliament is cried out on' by the common people as a result, with incredulous shouts of 'What, not keep Christmas? Here's a Reformation indeed!'

So strong was the popular attachment to the old festivities that many pro-Christmas riots occurred, threatening local tradesmen who had dared to open their shops on Christmas Day. In London, a crowd of apprentices assembled at Cornhill on 25 December, and there, 'in despite of authority, they set up Holly and Ivy' on the pinnacles of the public water conduit. When the Lord Mayor dispatched officers 'to pull down these gawds', the apprentices resisted them, forcing the mayor to break up the demonstration by force.

The worst disturbances took place at Canterbury, where a crowd of protestors first smashed up the shops that had been opened on Christmas Day and then went on to seize control of the entire city. This riot helped to pave the way for a major insurrection in Kent in 1648 that itself formed part of the 'Second Civil War' – a scattered series of risings against Parliament and in favour of the King, which Generals Fairfax and Cromwell only managed to suppress with great difficulty.

Parliamentary soldiers removed evergreen decorations from St Margaret's Church at Westminster and other churches in London. They destroyed the famous Glastonbury Thorn, a tree believed to have sprung on Christmas Day from the staff of Joseph of Arimathea, the uncle of Jesus Christ and legendary founder of Glastonbury Abbey. The Thorn traditionally flowered twice a year, at Easter and Christmas, and people flocked to watch these miraculous events. Cromwell's men deplored this ancient superstition, and burnt the tree.

By Christmas 1648, King Charles I was a prisoner of the English parliamentary army. He was executed in January 1649 and his body laid to rest at St George's Chapel, Windsor Castle, where he had kept his last Christmas. For ordinary people, celebrating Christmas would now become even harder.

Specific penalties were imposed on anyone found holding or attending a Christmas church service and public notices were nailed to trees forbidding the observation of Christmas. Although in theory it had been abolished, clandestine religious services marking Christ's Nativity continued to be held, and the secular pleasures of the season were covertly enjoyed, as far as people were able to do so. In his pamphlet *The Vindication of Christmas* (1652), John Taylor provided a lively portrait of how, he claimed, the old Christmas festivities were still being kept up by the farmers of Devon.

Following Cromwell's installation as Lord Protector in 1653, the celebration of Christmas continued to be proscribed. It is evident that Cromwell and senior members of his regime supported the prohibition, frequently transacting government business on 25 December as if it were a day just like any other.

The diarist John Evelyn searched in vain for Christmas Day services in the 1650s and had to celebrate at home. In 1657, though he managed to attend a service in London, soldiers surrounded the chapel and arrested everyone inside. Two of the most important major generals of the Protectorate, Goffe and Whalley, came to interrogate the miscreants, who were accused of 'observing the superstitious time of the Nativity' and praying for the King. Some of those arrested were sent to prison.

The wassail toast, deemed too secular, was also frowned upon.

One William Slater tried to replace the old carols with *Certain of David's Psalms intended for Christmas Carols*, which featured 'the most solemn tunes'. The Puritans complained that their legislation was being popularly ignored, but to no avail: the people's delight in Christmas traditions simply could not be extinguished.

## Old customs revived

*'I sent for a mince pie abroad'*

Although the Puritans had banned plum pudding – 'that broth of abominable things' – and Nativity pies, the latter soon reappeared, much smaller in size and without the cribs, to be renamed mince pies.

In 1660, with the restoration of Charles II to the throne, anti-Christmas legislation was soon swept away, to widespread joy. Although many of the old carols did not survive the Cromwellian period, or were forgotten until the Victorians revived them, both the religious and the secular elements of the full twelve days could once again be celebrated openly.

In his diaries, Samuel Pepys describes how he and his wife Elizabeth spent Christmas in the 1660s. On Christmas morning, Pepys went to church, where the pews were decorated with rosemary and ivy, while Elizabeth was often at home preparing dinner. On 25 December 1662, he left her 'not well' in bed. On his return, he sat at her bedside eating 'a mess of brave plum-porridge and a roasted pullet [young hen] … and I sent for a mince pie abroad, my wife not being well to make any herself'. But it's clear that Twelfth Night was the high point for the couple, with singing, dancing, drinking, and games like blind man's bluff. Pepys would sometimes hire a fiddler to entertain his friends, and he made sure there were 'good fires and candles' in his house. Then there was the cutting and eating of the Twelfth Night cake, which must have been important to him, because in 1668, he spent twenty shillings on the ingredients alone. For Pepys, Twelfth Night was also a time for reflection and thanks, 'This night making an end wholly of Christmas, with a mind fully satisfied with the great pleasures we have had … So home to supper and to bed, blessing God for His mercy …'

The Parliamentarians had perceived Christmas and other cherished old customs to be a threat, although they admitted that 'grand festivals and lesser holy-days … are the main things which the more ignorant and common sort among them do fight for'. They associated Christmas customs not only with Catholicism but also with the Royalist cause. But in the end, the Puritans did themselves and their cause no favours with ordinary folk by attacking the popular customs and celebration. In fact, they succeeded in alienating large numbers from their own repressive regime.

Puritan influence had a stronger hold in North America. In Boston, for example, up until 1681, you could be fined five shillings for simply showing 'Christmas spirit'! The feast, perceived as an unwelcome English tradition, also fell into decline after the American Revolution, and it would not be an official holiday in America until 1870.

# 5 January
## The Twelfth Day of Christmas

# BABY-CAKE

Twelfth Night cake

Now, now the mirth comes
With  Nthe cake full of plums,
Where bean's the king of the sport here;
Beside, we must know
The pea also
Must revel as queen in the court here.

Begin then to choose,
This night, as ye use,
Who shall for the present delight here;
Be a king by the lot,
And who shall not
Be Twelve-day queen for the night here!

Which known, let us make
Joy-sops with the cake;
And let not a man then be seen here,
Who unurged will not drink,
To the base from the brink,
A health to the king and the queen here!

Next crown the bowl full
With gentle lamb's wool,
And sugar, nutmeg, and ginger,
With store of ale, too;
And this ye must do
To make the wassail a swinger.

Give then to the king

And queen, wassailing,

And though with ale ye be wet here,

Yet part ye from hence

As free from offence

As when ye innocent met here.

Robert Herrick, 'Twelfth Night, or King and Queen'

# Twelfth Night cake

*'Of Twelfth-tide cakes, of peas and beans'*

Christmas culminated in Twelfth Night, a time of great celebration, involving feasts, games and the staging of plays. If friends and relations had gone home after the earlier festivities, they all came surging back for the culmination of the Yuletide season.

Twelfth Night was magnificently celebrated at court. There were 'divers interludes, rich masques and disports, and after that a great banquet' at which, in 1532, two hundred dishes were served, and temporary kitchens had had to be erected in the grounds of Greenwich Palace, so that the Master Cooks could make jellies and gingerbread. Elizabeth I had her own gingerbread maker, who created gingerbread figures in the Queen's likeness and those of her guests and visiting foreign dignitaries, to whom they were given out.

In 1552, Sir William Petre hosted a hundred guests at Ingatestone Hall, Essex, and feasted them on a whole sheep, a sucking pig, fifteen beef joints, sixteen raised pies, or 'coffins', pork, veal, geese, partridge, teal, capons, rabbits and larks. Lamb's wool was drunk from a bowl that was passed around among the company, each guest taking a sip.

For the sumptuous banquet that marked Twelfth Night, an enormous cake was traditionally baked, containing dried fruit, flour, honey and spices. Inside the cake were a coin or a bean as well as a pea, and slices were offered to guests as they arrived, men and women taking them from the right and left respectively; the lucky man and woman who found the coin or bean and the pea would be King and Queen of the Bean or Pea for the evening and be hoisted shoulder high to chalk crosses on the ceiling beams to ward off 'cursed devils, sprites and bugs, of conjuring and charms'. They would then lead the singing, dancing or disports. From payments made beforehand, it appears that at court the lucky recipients were often selected in advance, just to be on the safe side. In the nineteenth century, the Victorians would hark back to this tradition, adding silver charms or coins to their Christmas pudding. Sadly, no recipe for Twelfth Night cake survives from before 1803.

# Twelfth Night at court

*'A health to the king and the queen here!'*

In 1494, Henry VII and Elizabeth of York presided 'with great solemnity' over the festivities at Westminster Palace, and at 11 p.m., after divine service, they went in procession to Westminster Hall, where they and their guests, including the Lord Mayor and aldermen of London, were treated to an interlude performed by the King's players; 'but ere they had finished came in riding one of the King's Chapel', the composer and dramatist William Cornish, 'apparelled after the figure of St George; and after followed a fair virgin attired like unto a king's daughter and leading by a silken lace a terrible and huge red dragon, the which, in sundry places of the hall as he passed, spit fire at his mouth'. When Cornish came before the King, he declaimed a ballad, then began singing an anthem to St George, joined by the King's Chapel, who 'sang out with lusty courage. In pastime whereof the said Cornish avoided with the dragon, and the virgin was led unto the Queen's standing', to be taken under Elizabeth's protection.

Then there appeared 'twelve gentlemen leading by kerchiefs of pleasance twelve ladies, all goodly disguised, having before them a small tabor and a subtle fiddle, the which gentlemen leaped and danced all the length of the hall as they came, and the ladies slid after them', looking as if 'they stood upon a frame running'. When they came before the King, they danced for an hour, and 'it was wonderful to behold the exceeding leaps'.

The King and Queen then entertained their guests to a private banquet, seating them, at the King's direction, at 'a table of stone garnished with napery, lights and other necessaries'. Presently the disguised gentlemen came in 'bearing every each of them a dish, and after them as many knights and esquires as made the full number of sixty, the which sixty dishes were all served to the King, and as many served unto the Queen'. All the dishes were 'confections of sundry fruits and conserves, and so soon as the King and the Queen and the other estates were served, then was brought unto the Mayor's stage twenty-four dishes of the same manner service, with sundry wines and ale in most plenteous wise. And finally, as all worldly pleasure hath an end, the board was reverently withdrawn, and the King and Queen with the other estates, with a great sort of lights [were] conveyed into the palace.' The Lord Mayor did not get home until daybreak.

Twelfth Night was the last night on which the Lord of Misrule held sway, so the festivities were appropriately riotous. It was especially a time when normal rules and self-control did not apply – a period of deliberate inversion and misrule. As Shakespeare's Feste declares in *Twelfth Night*: 'Foolery, sir, does walk about the orb like the sun, it shines everywhere.'

In 1564, Mary, Queen of Scots, deliberately devised her Twelfth Night celebrations to outdo Queen Elizabeth's, and 'abdicated' so that two of her four maids, who were all called Mary, could share the role of Queen of the Bean. 'My pen staggereth,' wrote an English envoy, 'my hand faileth, further to write. The queen of the bean was that day in a gown of cloth of silver; her head, her neck, her shoulders, the rest of her whole body, so beset with stones, that more in our whole jewel-house were not to be found.'

In England, after the King and Queen had banqueted in the hall, the Lord Steward and the Treasurer of the Household would enter with their staves of office, bearing gold wassail cups containing a kind of mulled fruit punch that was drunk to toast the festive season. The steward would cry, 'Wassail! Wassail! Wassail!' and the choristers of the King's Chapel, waiting at the side of the hall, would 'answer with a good song'. The wassail cup was presented to the King and Queen and then passed around the table.

# Christmas ends

*'Down with the holly, ivy, all'*

Some thought it bad luck to leave Christmas decorations up after midnight on Twelfth Night, when the power of the Christ Child no longer held sway, for if the greenery was not put outside again, the tree spirits would bring disaster to the household in the coming year. But in some places, right up till the nineteenth century, the decorations were not taken down until Candlemas, 2 February, when Jesus was presented in the Temple on the feast of the Purification of the Virgin Mary. Robert Herrick warned of what might happen if the decorations were not removed:

> Down with the rosemary, and so
> Down with the bays and mistletoe;

Down with the holly, ivy, all
Wherewith ye decks the Christmas hall;
That so the superstitious find
Not one least branch there left behind:
For look! How many leaves there be
Neglected there (maids, trust to me),
So many goblins you shall see.

When the Yule log was finally allowed to burn itself out at the end of the Christmas season, people would save a piece of it to light next year's log, and keep some of its ashes in the house to protect against fire, lightning and toothache. The rest were used as fertiliser. Again, Herrick describes the custom:

Kindle the Christmas brand, and then
Till sunset let it burn;
Which quench'd, then lay it up again
Till Christmas next return.

Part must be kept wherewith to tend
The Christmas log next year.
And where 'tis safely kept, the fiend
Can do no mischief there.

End now the white-loaf and the pie,
And let all sports with Christmas die.

6 January

Epiphany

# AND THUS
# IT ENDED

The Yule Log burns out

The Wise Men's day here followeth, who out from Persia far,
Brought gifts and presents unto Christ, conducted by a star.
The Papists do believe that these were kings, and so them call,
And do affirm that of the same there were but three in all.
Here sundry friends together come, and meet in company,
And make a king amongst themselves by voice or destiny;
Who, after princely guise, appoints his officers alway,
Then unto feasting do they go, and long time after play:
Upon their boards, in order thick, their dainty dishes stand,
Till that their purses empty be and creditors at hand.
Their children herein follow them, and choosing princes here,
With pomp and great solemnity, they meet and make good cheer
With money either got by stealth, or of their parents eft [again],
That so they may be trained to know both riot here and theft.
Then, also, every householder, to his ability,
Doth make a mighty cake that may suffice his company:
Herein a penny doth he put, before it comes to fire,
This he divides according as his household doth require;
And every piece distributeth, as round about they stand,
Which in their names unto the poor is given out of hand.
But whoso chanceth on the piece wherein the money lies
Is counted king amongst them all, and is with shouts and cries
Exalted to the heavens up, who, taking chalk in hand,
Doth make a cross on every beam and rafters as they stand:
Great force and power have these against all injuries and harms,
Of cursed devils, sprites and bugs, of conjurings and charms,
So much this king can do, so much the crosses bring to pass,
Made by some servant, maid or child, or by some foolish ass!

Thomas Kirchmaier, 1553

fter the birth of Christ, the Three Wise Men, having
seen the star, set out toward... his birth, and their
arrival, said to have taken place... Jesus... 
celebrated as the feast of the Epiphany... 
a moment of sudden revelation or... the feast of
the Epiphany, gold, frankincense and myrrh were offered on the
royal household on behalf of the King... this ceremony
continues today, and is performed by the... on
behalf of the sovereign, in the Chapel Royal... 
Pageants were often staged to celebrate... 
the Epiphany were put on in London... 
in churches and churchyards and were... 
streets. Plays featuring the Three Kings were... 
celebrated of all pageants and... 
or financed by the goldsmiths' guild, called 'the Feast of
the Star', depicting the coming of the...

fter the birth of Christ, the three wise men, having seen the star, set out to find the new King, and their arrival, said to have been twelve days later, was celebrated as the feast of the Epiphany, which means a moment of sudden revelation or manifestation. On the feast of the Epiphany, gold, frankincense and myrrh were offered in the royal chapels on behalf of the King or Queen. The ceremony continues today, and is performed by the Bishop of London, on behalf of the sovereign, in the Chapel Royal at St James's Palace.

Pageants were often staged at court. Mystery plays acting out the Epiphany were put on in hundreds of English towns; at first in churches and churchyards, and later on wagons that toured the streets. Plays featuring the three kings were some of the most celebrated of all pageants and, appropriately, were produced or financed by the goldsmiths' guild. One, called 'The Feast of the Star', depicting the coming of the Magi, was presented in churches, with a star on a mechanical pulley being used to guide the wise men to the Christ Child. In most of the plays the three kings find Jesus in a stable, but in others He is in a house or 'halle'. The Christ Child is referred to by a variety of beautiful names in these pageants, of which 'Lily Flower' in the York Cycle 'Three Kings Play' is the most poetic.

It was in Victorian times that English schoolchildren began to act in Nativity plays in which the three kings featured prominently.

Epiphany celebrations could equal or rival those of Christmas Day itself. It was the final opportunity of the season to make merry and indulge in feasting, revelry and disguisings. Roast lamb was traditionally served, and people ate up the remains of the Twelfth Night cake, or an Epiphany tart made in the shape of a star, filled with a variety of jams. The festival reached its apotheosis in the late seventeenth century, with large iced cakes topped with sugar figures of the Magi being consumed at the evening revels, and delightful chasing, kissing and guessing games played.

For most, Epiphany was the last great day of processions, feasts, festivity and fun. The Yule log burned until the end, and spicy foods (representing the Eastern Magi) were part of the feast. Epiphany marked the end of Christmastide. At court, the Yuletide season officially ended on 2 February with the solemn celebration of Candlemas, the feast of the Purification of the Virgin Mary, when the King and Queen went in procession to Mass. On this feast day, the churches were ablaze with candles and packed with worshippers.

Christmas was coming to an end, and it was time to clean up the mess, get back to work, and settle down to normal life. Some years, Plough Monday fell on 7 January, which was known as St Distaff's Day, or Rock Day, both a distaff and a rock being alternative names for a spindle, for it was on this day that women resumed their domestic duties. 'It stoppeth a gap [and] saveth a woman from being idle,' Anthony Fitzherbert wrote rather primly in his *Boke of Husbandrie* in 1523. Then, as now, as Robert Herrick describes, people began to get ready to go back to work:

Partly work and partly play
Ye must, on St Distaff's day;
From the plough soon free your team,
Then come home and fodder them;
If the maids a-spinning go,
Burn the flax and fire the tow.
Bring in pails of water then,
Let the maids bewash the men.
Give St Distaff all the right,
Then bid Christmas sport good night,
And next morrow every one
To his own vocation.

On Plough Monday, before the Reformation, it was customary for farmers and those who owned shares in a communal plough, to drag it from door to door in the village or hamlet, craving blessings for it and donations for the parish. Anyone refusing risked having his garden ploughed over. Edward VI banned the tradition.

Christmas had survived the tumultuous years of Reformation and Puritan rule, as an ancient respite of warmth and pleasure in the bleakest time of winter. In the twenty-first century, we can still recognise much of the Tudor Christmas, although Christmas cards, Christmas crackers, Christmas trees, Santa Claus and the commercialisation of the season were all a long way in the future. Queen Victoria, Prince Albert and Charles Dickens reinvented Christmas, as a family celebration, in the nineteenth century.

If you want to get a real sense of a Tudor Christmas, you can visit Hampton Court Palace in December and walk through the cloisters. Beneath leaded windows you will see the traditional greenery of the season, entwined with dried fruit, berries and candles.

Nothing is more evocative of a Tudor Christmas than the natural decorations of evergreens and the ancient Christmas scents of cinnamon, ginger, cloves and nutmeg mingled with oranges, pine and juniper. All just as it was five hundred years ago, when Tudor monarchs kept Christmas there.

Now, good cheer, and welcome, and God be with you, and I thank
you!

Nicholas Breton, *Fantasticks*, 1626

# SELECT BIBLIOGRAPHY

Arbeau, Thoinot: *Orchésographie* (Langres, 1589)

Archer, Jeremy: *A Royal Christmas* (London, 2012)

Brears, Peter: *All the King's Cooks* (London, 1999)

Breton, Nicholas: *Fantasticks* (London, 1626)

Breverton, Terry: *The Tudor Kitchen* (Stroud, 2015)

Burton, Elizabeth: *The Early Tudors at Home* (London, 1976)

Carter, Simon: *Christmas Past, Christmas Present: Four Hundred Years of English Seasonal Customs, 1600–2000* (Geffrye Museum Trust, 1997)

Craig, Elizabeth: *English Royal Cookbook* (London, 1953, 1998)

Deegan, Alan, and Smith-Howard, Alycia: *The Food of Love: The Taste of Shakespeare in Four Seasons* (Cwmbach, 2012)

Dodd, A. H.: *Elizabethan England* (London, 1961)

Doran, Gregory: *The Shakespeare Almanac* (London, 2009)

Durston, Chris: 'The Puritan War on Christmas' (*History Today*, 1985)

*Elinor Fettiplace's Receipt Book* (ed. Hilary Spurling, London, 1986 [1604])

Emmison, F. G.: *Tudor Food and Pastimes* (London, 1964)

Evelyn, John: *The Diary of John Evelyn* (Woodbridge, 1995)

*A Golden Christmas Treasury* (ed. Mark Daniel, London, 1989)

Goodman, Ruth: *How to be a Tudor* (London, 2015)

Groom, Susanne: *At the King's Table: Royal Dining Through the Ages* (London, 2013)

Herrick, Robert: *Hesperides* (London, 1648)

—*Now, Now the Mirth Comes: Christmas Poetry by Robert Herrick* (ed. Douglas D. Anderson, Morrisville, 2007)

Hopley, Claire: *The History of Christmas Food and Feast* (Barnsley, 2009)

Hutton, Robert: *The Rise and Fall of Merry England: The Ritual Year in Tudor England* (Oxford, 1994)

Jackson, Sophie: *The Medieval Christmas* (Stroud, 2005)

Kelleher, Susan, and Rodgers, Rene: *A Christmas Miscellany* (English Heritage, 2007)

Kirchmaier, Thomas: *Regnum Papisticum* (Basel, 1553)

Laslett, Peter: *The World We Have Lost: Further Explored* (London, 2015)

Markham, Gervase: *The English Housewife* (London, 1615)

Moon, Jim: 'Christmas Spirits: The Origin of Ghost Stories at Christmas' (www.hypnogoria.com)

Mortimer, Ian: *The Time Traveller's Guide to Elizabethan England* (London, 2012)

*The Oxford Book of Carols* (ed. Percy Dearmer, R. Vaughan Williams and Martin Shaw, Oxford, 1928, 1964)

Paston-Williams, Sarah: *The Art of Dining: A History of Cooking and Eating* (London, 1995)

Pepys, Samuel: *The Diaries of Samuel Pepys – A Selection* (London, 2003)

*Piae Cantiones ecclesiasticae et scholasticae veterum episcoporum* (*Pious ecclesiastical and school songs of the ancient bishops*) (Greifswald, 1582)

Plowden, Alison: *Elizabethan England* (London, 1982)

*A Proper New Book of Cookery* (London, 1575)

Pyatt, Wendy: 'A Tudor Christmas' (www.localhistories.org)

*A Right Royal Christmas: An Anthology* (compiled Hugh Douglas, Stroud, 2001)

Rowse, A. L.: *The Elizabethan Renaissance: The Life of the Society* (London, 1971)

Salzman, L. F.: *England in Tudor Times* (London, 1926)

*Shakespeare's England* (by the editors of *Horizon* magazine, London, 1964)

Sim, Alison: *Food and Feast in Tudor England* (Stroud, 1997)

Stow, John: *A Survey of London* (London, 1598; Stroud, 1994)

*Tottel's Miscellany* (ed. H. E. Rollins, Cambridge, Mass., 1965)

Trueman, C. N.: 'Tudor Christmas' (www.historylearningsite.co.uk)

Tusser, Thomas: *Five Hundred Points of Good Husbandry* (London, 1573)

Youings, Joyce: *Sixteenth Century England* (London, 1984)

Weir, Alison: *Henry VIII: King and Court* (London, 2001)

— *Elizabeth the Queen* (London, 1998)

Winterson, Jeanette: *Christmas Days* (London, 2016)